EDUCATION WARRIOR

A MEMOIR OF MORRIS CUTLER

BY

DIANE CUTLER LEWIS

Education Warrior
A Memoir of Morris Cutler

Solutions Press
ISBN: 978-0-9996497-5-6
First Edition: September 2019

This is a work of non-fiction. The opinions expressed in this book are those of the author alone.

CONTENTS

MORRIS CUTLER SCHOLARSHIP FUND

EDUCATION WARRIORS

A Non-Profit Organization

Every child deserves a quality education. Education unites the world. We're all warriors at heart, and collectively, we CAN make a difference.

In honor of Morris Cutler, I created a non-profit, **Education Warriors** to provide tutoring scholarships to deserving youth from all backgrounds.

The more money we raise, the more students get academic assistance.

Your generous donation, whether $10 or $10,000, empowers students to stay in school, go to college, and build a better tomorrow.

"Be the change you wish to see in the world." Gandhi

To donate go to
www.EducationWarrior.org

DEDICATION

If every child grew up with parents like mine

the world would be a better place.

Dedicated to Morris and Faye Cutler

PROLOGUE

"Did you find everything you need?" asked the young woman assisting me in the store.

"I recognize your accent. Where are you from originally?"

"I'm from Afghanistan," she replied.

My heart swelled with excitation.

"I graduated high school in Kabul during the 1970s."

"Why were you there?

"My father wrote the first Royal Afghan Curriculum to teach students to read, write and learn about their country."

She tilted her head, thought for a moment. "I think I learned to read with those books." She smiled. I smiled. We bonded.

I handed her my card. "I'm writing a book and would love to hear your story."

The young woman shared that the Taliban killed her father in the late 1990s when she was five years old leaving her family traumatized with no income. Her mother, terrified she and her children would be next, fled on foot through the jagged Hindu Kush Mountains. After a month-long journey, barely alive, they took refuge in a camp just inside the Pakistani border. They joined tens of thousands of other escapees, who left their homeland to search for freedom. There, she learned to read and write Dari using precious twenty-year-old textbooks others carried with them out of the country.

I realized Dad's work survived decades of destruction, lived on to prepare this young Afghan woman to attend college in the United States of America. My father, Morris Cutler became a catalyst to bring literacy to a nation and beyond.

Education Warrior is an inspirational memoir of how one man affected millions. Not many can claim this accomplishment. I hope this book inspires you to accomplish greatness with your life too.

ACKNOWLEDGEMENTS

Aunt Ruth, thank you for inspiring me to write this book.

Wes Beavis friend, speaker, author, your encouragement to write daily thoughts and experiences launched a worthy book.

I'm grateful for my biggest cheerleaders, family and friends who knew my father.

Jeanne Bickford and Katheren Dickinson, "The Lettuce Leaf Ladies". Writing, reading and salads at each gathering spurred me on to complete the project.

Katheren, you taught me how to find my voice.

Randy Rosenthal, your keen sense helped shape and mold the story.

Elaine Duroff and Norm Bour you courageously gave honest, constructive feedback.

Lee Pound, chief editor, THANK YOU! You saw a bigger vision for the book than I did. Your expertise is invaluable to the creation of Education Warrior.

1

AFGHANISTAN, FULL CIRCLE

The smell of fresh ink permeated the classroom. The headmaster asked the students to line up, opened the mysterious box on his desk, raised two crisp new textbooks high over his head like trophies. The students cheered.

One at a time, he handed out the textbooks. Each student bowed their head, accepted the book, clutched it to their chests like an irreplaceable treasure, and scurried back to their seats. They slipped their nervous fingers between each page, leaned in close, breathed in the unfamiliar pleasant aroma of the pages, took in every detail, every word, every image.

For most of these children, this textbook represented the first time in their lives they'd not only handled but taken a textbook home to study.

The United States Agency for International Development (USAID) funded the project responsible for these books, designed to bring Afghanistan, a stagnant, isolated country, out of the Middle Ages into a Western-oriented world. My father, Morris Cutler, led this monumental challenge.

On September 3, 1973, my family arrived in Kabul, Afghanistan for a two-year stay to support Dad's assignment to create a formalized reading program, The Royal Curriculum of Afghanistan.

Before we arrived, education in Afghanistan was limited to memorizing verses from the Quran. A team of Afghan educators worked with Dad to write a series of textbooks for grades one through six for the Afghan government. The team translated the reading books into two main languages, Dari and Pashtu, and distributed hundreds of thousands of them to new schools around the country. These texts helped a new generation of children become literate.

Back in the States four years later (1979) I watched the BBC World News report the Russian invasion of Afghanistan. I watched tanks roll through the streets and bonfires consume hundreds of thousands of confiscated textbooks along the Kabul River. With tears running down my cheeks, I called my parents to tell Dad about the news. He and I watched the Soviet troops destroy the opus he had worked hard to build. His efforts seemed irretrievably lost.

After decades of hearing bad news about Afghanistan, in April 2002, a few months after 9/11, when the US went to war against the Taliban, I received an unexpected call from an old school friend, Chris Brown, my classmate from the American International School of Kabul (AISK).

After a few minutes of excited chatter, we discovered our careers mirrored our parents. My tutoring business followed in my father's education-oriented footsteps. Chris became a Foreign Service officer for the US government like his father.

"The State Department hired me to lead the Crisis Task Force for Reconstruction in Afghanistan with USAID," Chris said. "That's the same agency your father worked for. Seems speaking fluent Dari and Urdu is suddenly in demand again. That's what I get for growing up in Afghanistan and Pakistan."

I peppered him with questions about our decades ago foreign home.

"Is Kabul recognizable today?"

In a sad, deflated voice, he said, "No. The Soviet invaders flattened both our homes. Our school became a Soviet military camp in the late seventies. When the Taliban took control in the nineties, it became their base. After the invasion in 2002, the government turned the school into an orphanage for children who lost their parents.

"Life in Afghanistan reverted to barbaric ways, women and children tortured, and a decent education impossible," he said. "I called to give you the latest news."

I hadn't talked to Chris since our college years, readied myself to hear awful or wonderful news. My silence gave him permission to continue.

"Afghan tribes are known for their tenacity. You won't believe what happened."

"Tell me."

"First the US State Department received an urgent fax from Acting President Karzai, sent on InterContinental Hotel letterhead in January 2002.

"After the Taliban bombed the Ministry of Education building in Kabul, the hotel remained the only safe place to work. The fax asked President Bush for assistance to rewrite the national textbooks. Karzai wanted to re-enroll children in new schools after *Nowruz,* the Afghan New Year celebration. They needed five million new books on hand when the schools reopened in March."

I asked, "What national textbooks? Didn't you say they destroyed all Dad's books?"

Chris said, "Yes, the Russians burned most of the books. The Taliban finished the job. Whoever ran the country at the time mutilated then rewrote the surviving books. The Mujahedeen wrote the names of their tribal ancestors over the names of the Afghan national heroes in the stories your father wrote. The Taliban forbade pictures of faces in the textbooks. We found simple sketches in the primary books your dad wrote of a female teacher who wore a scarf over her head teaching children near the blackboard—but they scratched out the faces. Fundamental belief required them to admire or worship no one but Allah. I also noticed in one first grade book on counting they scribbled out sketches of melons and drew Kalashnikov rifles instead."

"The Taliban brainwashed little boys to believe in violence and war?" I asked

"Also, we believed they destroyed every copy of your Dad's textbooks. We thought we needed to start over with a deadline less than three months away. Because travel was still dangerous, I flew into Islamabad and my staff and I drove to the tent camps at Peshawar, Pakistan, which housed more than a million people, almost as big as Las Vegas. These refugees fled on foot through the treacherous Khyber Pass, carried all their belongings. Many toted their beloved textbooks. NGOs (Non-Governmental Organizations) such as Save the Children and Doctors Without Borders helped these families survive.

"Your dad would have been so disappointed because these simple paperback books were a disaster. We got to work. Over the next 24 hours, my staff recruited 10 top educators from the refugee camps, all with master's degrees or above from foreign universities who had returned to contribute to rebuilding Afghanistan. Four of the 10 were women!"

"Dad will love hearing that."

"The next morning, as my driver transported me to the guest house we were using as our headquarters, I prayed for guidance on the specific directions I would give the educators. Washington officials wanted all extremist ideology removed from the books. To me, that was promoting hate from a different angle by imposing U.S. politics onto Afghan children. Your father wrote the books to promote Afghan pride and patriotism."

"Yes, he did."

"That morning, I stood in front of the group in our makeshift office and gave them three simple directives based on the idea that no Afghan student deserves to be told to hate another person, country, or political view.

"First, we remove statements of that nature and teach children to embrace others, no matter their religious belief, ethnic origin, gender, or color of skin. Every religion on earth teaches this.

"Second, we say that no group, women, Pashtun, Kuchi, Hazaras, Russian, or American, is superior to another. Each person has value, no matter their gender or cultural origin.

"Third, restate passages that suggest hatred for another country and instead show interest in and discovery of other lands."

"Dad will be so proud of you!"

"Thank you," Chris said. "When I finished outlining our plan of action, I stood in silence, gazing into the eyes of these humble educators. Each had their own harrowing escape to share. After what seemed like minutes, but I knew to be only seconds, the team stood and applauded. Most had tears in their eyes, and I too, was overcome with emotion. One gentleman yelled out in Dari. 'Chrisjan, we are here to help! Change our return ride to midnight and we will begin tomorrow at 6 am!'" The others agreed.

"There's more," Chris said, "your dad will love this part. Dozens of the original textbooks survived too. Families hid them in walls, in dirt floors, under carpets. The Taliban refused to give girls an education. Their mothers created covert groups of ten or fifteen, who met in secret. Although the penalty if caught was public stoning, mothers taught their daughters the forbidden arts of reading and writing. Those who possessed one precious book shared it. A generation of girls became literate in Dari and Pashtu with your father's books."

I felt chills.

"Diane, we found the original printing press, later the plates. Afghan teachers concealed them. Afghans moved both ways across the Pakistani border for thirty years.

Chris told me that since the book modification would take at least two weeks, he flew to Kabul to meet with the Education

Minister. The fifth day after his arrival, he received a call on his satellite phone. I listened as he recounted the conversation.

"Through the crackling transmission, I heard the voice on the other end say, 'The books have been completed!'

"'What? You're sure two people read through each book?'

"'Yes, yes, Chrisjan,' replied the master teacher. 'We have two highlight colors in each book. I checked them all myself. We need you back in Peshawar!'

"In amazement," Chris said, "I shared the news with the Minister of Education, who was seated in front of me. The following day, I hitched a ride back to Peshawar on a United Nations flight."

"Incredible," I said.

"We can accomplish wonders when we focus on the mission," Chris said. "The next phase was to coordinate printing contracts in Pakistan. One company couldn't fill the entire order before *Nowruz* so I spent days in intense negotiations in three languages: Urdu to Dari, Dari to English, back and forth, back and forth. My head ached by the end of each day, but what a rush! The mission was crazy and amazing at the same time! In the tiny guest house, artists redrew faces back into the sketches for each of the master textbooks while calligraphers hand wrote the final drafts for 200 books! Picture this. We had one table in the guest house, so most editors transferring them sat in circles, barefoot on the floor, all dressed in *shalwars*. Remember the puffy pants and long shirts?"

"Of course, I still have two outfits packed away."

"Cute," Chris laughed. "The men wore colorful skull caps depicting their tribe. The women concealed their entire bodies with western clothing and wore simple white head scarves. None wore their *chadres* (burkas). Within the circle, piles and piles of books overflowed in front of them as they worked into the night."

"What an incredible scene!"

"It began with your dad creating and writing the books with his team all those years ago," Chris said. "Because the original masters from the 1970s were printed from giant sheets of waxed paper, calligraphers worked day and night cutting and pasting everything by hand. Then they flash photographed the waxed sheets using the old version of printing. What a laborious process." Chris' voice grew more animated. "The local presses in Peshawar ran round the clock at full speed. We farmed out the majority of the printing to larger companies in Lahore and Karachi. Within a week or two, Pakistani *lorries* (trucks) were lining up in front of the warehouse we rented at the Peshawar Airport. Boxes of textbooks arrived daily, first hundreds then thousands and hundreds of thousands. What a marvelous sight!"

"Five million children needed books," I said. "That's a daunting task. Dad used to say, 'Teaching a person to read and think is the ultimate gift of liberty.' Now I know why he cared so much."

"So true," Chris said. "At the airport, we hired teams of Afghans to sort the books into kits, creating enormous bundles for each school in designated regions: Dari versions for the central and northern regions and Pashtu translations for the southeast. I flew back to Washington, D.C. to arrange air transport for the books. We're talking millions of dollars from our State Department. The United States Air Force handled a portion of the airlift and, in an ironic twist, private Russian cargo planes contracted for the remainder."

Within days, crews delivered over five million brand new textbooks. Afghan teachers and children rejoiced as they received new books for the first time in over 30 years. Chris and his team met the goal. Hamid Karzai, the acting president of Afghanistan, felt proud that he put Afghan children back in school.

I listened to Chris, visualized a far bigger historic movement than Dad imagined. My father accepted his assignment back in the 1970s to join people together, broaden educational growth in Afghanistan, help Afghan children learn to think, and build a better tomorrow for their country. At the time, we didn't know the enormous impact of Dad's work.

Chris said, "Diane, of all the projects I've worked on around the world, this one gives me the most gratification. I couldn't wait to share the news."

"I'm happy you did. When we hang up, I'll call Dad."

"You know I'm a huge fan of your father."

"Thank you, I'll let him know Chris."

Tears of joy slipped down my checks. My body tingled. My father, Morris Cutler, created history. Although Dad said little about his accomplishments, his legacy outlasted war to shape the literacy of an entire nation for generations to come. I'm overwhelmed at what he achieved.

His story begins in the early 1900s, when his young parents escaped a violent civil war in Bolshevik Russia to search for a new better future in America.

2

THE OLD COUNTRY

My grandparents, Abe and Bella Kotlarski, Russian Jewish refugees, lived in Brusilov, a quaint village on the outskirts of Kiev, the capital of Ukraine. Abe, light brown curly hair, pale skin, deep blue eyes, stood no more than five feet four inches tall. Bella, with similar hair and eyes on a tiny four-foot nine-inch frame, could pass for his sister rather than his wife. Together, they made an adorable couple.

Aunt Mima Sarah and her husband Fatter Beryl Cohen, Dad's great aunt and uncle, were the first of his family to emigrate to the United States in 1904. Before the Russian Army drafted him, Fatter Beryl, a master baker, ran his Brusilov shop, frequented by friends and musicians. Abe and Bella patronized the bakery for many years, enjoyed the delicious aromas, mouth-watering strudel, *challah* (egg bread), poppyseed bread.

Beryl and Sarah's example encouraged Abe and Bella to dream of ways to leave their difficult life in Russia for the free land of America.

In 1914, World War I broke out. Later in the war, the Russians drafted my grandfather Abe into the army, which left Bella alone with their two young sons. For the next few years, while Abe fought in the war, German soldiers besieged Kiev, and nearby villages.

Young German soldiers occupied the Kotlarski's tiny home in Brusilov. At first, the soldiers' abrupt forcefulness frightened Bella but soon they helped her and her two babies. The soldiers shared food, water to keep them alive. Bella took refuge in the dark, stifling underground basement with her sons. Their lives depended on how well they stayed hidden. No law protected the territory. Russian hooligans killed Jews at random while German soldiers protected Bella.

After several weeks in the Kotlarski home, the German soldiers moved on, left Bella to fend for herself. She used every resource available to find scarce food. She yearned for Abe's return, hugged her babies to sleep each night, where they kept each other's bodies warm.

Scraps of wood gathered in the forest heated the house. Seated near the fire, she sewed. She experienced *nachas* (blessings) while she watched her sons play on the tattered hand-woven rug in the middle of the rustic room. Bella sold the clothes she made for money to buy food. She cooked on the small potbelly stove, which also warmed their two-room cottage.

Months passed. Bitter winter temperatures reached twenty degrees below zero. Due to scarce food supplies, Bella's two sons withered away, first one died, then the next. Bella, weakened from lack of food, had to be rescued, ended up in a filthy infirmary.

In early 1917, a popular rebellion drove Russia's Tsar Nicholas II out of office, kept Abe in the army. The new multi-party government continued the German war. The Germans repatriated Communist leader Vladimir Lenin to Russia to overthrow the interim government, sign a peace treaty, which happened in early 1918. After the Bolshevik Revolution, Russia's Communist-led government fought a brutal civil war for years. Germany sent their troops to the Western front to fight the British and French armies.

When the two governments signed the treaty, my grandfather Abe, grateful for his life after horrific battles, lay in an army hospital hundreds of miles from his family. Since mail didn't exist, Bella and Abe stayed out of touch, uncertain as to whether either survived the war. She prayed every night for God to bring him home.

Weeks later, discharged from the army because of a severe foot injury, Abe created a cane from a fallen tree branch, and began his long journey home to Brusilov. He hobbled on his injured left foot to avoid pressure on his swollen, lacerated toes since no train or bus transport existed. Abe wanted to find his wife Bella, whom he missed, his two sons, who he hoped remembered him.

The snow melted, turned to ice in the frigid night air. Spring emerged. Sprigs of green shot through patches of snow. The chill of winter filled the air. After he trekked on foot hundreds of miles over many weeks on his damaged foot, he saw his village, Brusilov, in the distance. A gust of wind whipped through the trees, sliced through the fabric of Abe's army uniform. To stay warm, he tucked his chin lower into the buttoned-up collar.

He approached the town, sickened from the devastation, ran like an injured deer shot in the hindquarters. His heart pounded, he searched through the ashes of his village for his loved ones. On one corner, he found the synagogue they once used for prayer, a pile of rubble.

When he arrived at their tiny home, he saw charred branches peek above gray ash around their tarnished potbelly stove. His mouth watered, a memory of his beloved wife Bella cooking delicious chicken soup. He sighed, relieved to see home again, disappointed to smell no familiar aromas, sense no sign of life, only memories.

Where's my family? Abe thought. Oblivious to his own injury, he ran outside. He sloshed through the icy mud, questioned the townspeople about his family. In this lawless ruin, nobody knew where his family ended up.

Hopeless, alone, Abe wandered, searched, until nightfall approached. Abe went to the local infirmary to get treatment for his injured foot. After they treated his injuries, disoriented from pain, he wandered into the women's quarter of the tiny hospital, glimpsed a familiar face in a distant bed.

"It's a miracle," he whispered. He hurried to the bed. Bella's tired eyes peered up at him, her mouth widened into a smile of joy. After she lost her two babies to starvation, she collapsed from grief. A stranger found her, brought her to the infirmary.

Thus began what my grandparents and father called "Cutler Luck." The reunion blended both joy, sadness. My grandparents survived their grief over the loss of their two sons, recounted their blessing to be together again.

For the next few months, Abe and Bella struggled to stay alive. Waves of marauders, Bolsheviks, White Russians, rampaged through town, looted everything of value, showed no respect for human life. Abe and Bella yearned to go to America.

A year later, through the HIAS Agency, an underground Jewish relief agency, my grandparents received money from Bella's brother, my great Uncle Banish, who prospered in St. Louis. This generous gift from Uncle Banish launched my grandparents' courageous journey to the United States.

In 1922, the family joined a clandestine group of refugees headed west for the Russian-Polish border. Esther, a stoic woman, traveled alongside them with her young daughter Bess, graceful like a tiny ballerina.

Let me explain the connection between Esther and Bess. When one of the marauders ravaged the territory, they burned Uncle Banish's first wife and children alive in the synagogue. Esther, the younger sister of Banish's first wife, lost her husband in the war, left them both widowed. They followed orthodox Jewish tradition. Uncle Banish agreed to marry Esther, accepted her young daughter Bess into his family. Together, they emigrated to the United States.

My grandparents made secret arrangements with the Jewish underground to lead them out of Russia. If military guards from either country spotted refugees, the soldiers shot them on the spot. To ensure their safety, the forty or more refugees traveled in the damp of night, hid among thick trees in the forest along the banks of the icy Dnieper River, crossed 300 miles to the Polish border.

Before they started the journey, the underground leaders told refugees to layer their clothes. They sewed food, money, jewelry into the lining of the garments, left all other possessions behind. Each adult carried a cloth knapsack filled with bread and cheese, in case they got separated from the group. The youngest child? Dad's three-month-old older brother Alex.

On the journey, Abe and Bella carried their precious little bundle, Alex. They journeyed by foot, close behind their guide, side-by-side with Esther and angelic little Bess. They bonded into one family, marched toward a common goal. Behind them, a few men walked backward, scouted for soldiers, used tree branches to sweep away footprints to leave no visible marks of their passage in the soil.

In the early morning of the journey's second week, two men, dressed in mud-spattered clothes from the nighttime dew, one much smaller than the other, ran out of the trees.

"It's a miracle!" Abe said. Ten-year-old Joe Kagan, their nephew, the eldest son of Banish, ran into his arms. They assumed the boy died! Joe looked frightened. Bella placed bundled-up Alex in Esther's arms, ran to hug her curly-headed nephew. Through his tears, little Joe told Bella how two years earlier, when marauders set the synagogue full of Jews on fire, he escaped into the woods, watched his family and the synagogue burn to the ground.

Days later, Joe said, a Russian woodcutter who lived in the forest found him, saw his trauma, raised him in the forest for two years. When the woodcutter heard the refugee group's escape plans, he encouraged Joe, age ten, to join them to seek a new life in America, unaware the group included Joe's relatives.

In joyful reunion, Bella and Abe offered their newfound nephew comfort, love, stability. Like many wartime children, Joe suffered horrific emotional trauma from the events he endured. The fears haunted him the rest of his life.

Weeks passed. The refugees made their cautious way northwest through thick forest toward the Polish border, their gateway to freedom. They slept by day, traveled on foot in the chilly nights, aware the most dangerous portion of their journey lay in the future, when they crossed the ice-cold Dnieper River patrolled by Russians on one side, Polish soldiers on the other. Unless they could cross the river in silence, they were doomed.

Hungry, exhausted from the long trek, the refugees reached the steep banks of the icy river on the edge of the forest, where they exchanged signals with the Polish underground liaison who waited to assist them. A cold layer of dense fog chilled the air. Hidden among the thick trees, a small wooden rowboat waited to ferry several of them across at a time. They waited more than a week for the bright full moon to dissolve into a crystal sliver in the black sky. When the moment came, they listened to their guide tell them in Russian, "If they hear or see one of you, we will all die."

Abe and Bella followed strict orders from their guides, took their long-awaited turn. Bess climbed aboard the rickety vessel with her mother Esther. Black *babushkas* (scarves) covered their heads. Bella, baby Alex, Abe, and ten-year-old Joe followed in silence. The boat creaked, sloshed at the muddy shore. A cold damp mist froze the dark air. No one spoke.

One guide pushed the boat from shore, the other plied the oars through the water without splashing. My Uncle Alex began to cry. The anguished guide whispered to Bella, "The baby's cries will alert the guards. They will kill us all! Drown the infant in the river!"

Esther grabbed Alex from a shocked Bella, smothered his cries in her coat, not knowing if he could breathe. A heart-pounding crossing followed. The guide rowed in silence for twenty minutes until they reached the Polish shore of the river. They watched for border guards, in silence climbed out of the boat, ran into the nearby woods.

Once concealed among the trees on Polish land, they caught their breath. Esther unfolded her coat, beamed a warm smile at baby Alex, who breathed in comfort. Bella and Abe embraced their son, thanked God for the miracle he bestowed on them.

Days later, they boarded a steamer out of Poland bound for New York Harbor, the safe haven where they dreamed of a new life free of religious persecution. Their dreams, to own a store, work together with orthodox Jews, and enjoy life with the family they loved.

It was customary to exempt first-class refugee passengers from European countries who arrived in New York Harbor from the inspection process at Ellis Island. In theory, if a person purchased a first or second-class ticket, they were less likely to become a public burden in America due to medical or legal problems.

Third class passengers, like my grandparents, faced a far different reception. They traveled in steerage, in crowded, unsanitary conditions near the bottom of the steamship, spent the rough two-week Atlantic crossing seasick in their bunks.

Weary from two weeks below deck, Abe, Bella, Alex rode the ferry to Ellis Island, joined other third-class immigrants for medical and legal inspections. They arrived on American soil October 1, 1923.

After they waited for hours in long lines, their turn arrived. The inspector scanned the ship's passenger manifest, filled out at the port of embarkation in Poland, found their name, Kotlarski in Russian. Since none of the officers at Ellis Island spoke Yiddish or Russian, the inspector wrote "Cutler" when he filled out their papers. My grandparents neither read nor wrote English, like many European immigrants in the early 1900s. With a nod from Abe and Bella to the immigration officer, their new American name, Cutler, replaced their old Russian last name, Kotlarski.

3

FIRST AMERICAN

Morrie at 2 years old

September 20, 1924. A loud wail echoed like a siren through the modest two-room apartment, alerted the world to the arrival of a spirited newborn, Morris Cutler. Abe cradled his tiny son, a proud beam glowed across his face. He leaned down, kissed Bella's moist forehead. Exhausted from childbirth, she smiled back. "He's beautiful," she said in Yiddish. They gave a blissful silent moment of thanks for their blessing, a healthy son God bestowed on their new lives in America.

4

BECOMING A MENSCH

The year before he started school, Morris tagged along with his mother to free adult English classes created to help immigrants adapt to their new country. Week after week, four-year-old Morrie listened to adult level language instruction, absorbed new vocabulary, and heard lessons in pronunciation, grammar, and spelling. Morrie sat quietly next to his mother in the adult-filled classroom, He felt special, grew to love the time with his mother while she learned English.

Two years later, young Morris hurried out of school, whispered his imaginary safety code into the rubber band on his wrist, pretended he possessed a two-way wrist radio like

Dick Tracy's. Detective Tracy, a brilliant plotter, inspired Morrie to learn to do the same.

Morrie loved Speckart's Drug Store, his private Treasure Island, where he got his fill of adventure with nary an ounce of danger to himself. Morrie, a scrappy, pleasant little fellow, irresistible dimples when he smiled, always stayed out of the way. Speckart's employees knew he enjoyed the superhero adventures, never complained about his lengthy visits after school, nor knew he imagined a far superior dream life, his personal version of superman.

Morrie as a child

In the 1930s, superheroes burst onto the scene from various planets and bizarre accidents. Morrie marveled at how these larger than life characters flew about in their quest to protect mankind. He drove his busy parents mad when he zoomed around the market in a red cape to mimic those flying crusaders. Though he couldn't fly on his own, the sight of planes overhead transfixed him. He vowed one day to learn to fly. His vivid imagination spurred him on. He turned the pages of the newest comic book, awestruck by noble characters ready to sacrifice their lives to save those they loved. These powerful men of fiction inspired Morrie to dream of a future in which he flew like a superhero, fought evil with every power he possessed.

At dinner one night, Morrie fidgeted in excited anticipation.

"What did you learn in school today?" his mother asked in Yiddish.

"This isn't from school, but I read about this swell spy plane in one of the new comics at Speckart's and I read in my new history book from Pop about an American plane, the Douglas World Cruiser, which flew around the whole globe," he said. "They left from Seattle in April, landed back in Seattle on September 28th, 1924, eight days after my birthday. Isn't that keen?"

Abe and Alex chuckled together over Morrie's youthful exuberance. Planes fascinated him from the day he first noticed odd objects in the sky. He raved about them every possible chance. From this enthusiastic fan, the whole family learned about the development of airplanes.

"Morris, I'm glad you read a lot but pay attention to me please. I asked you to tell us what you learned in *school*," Bella said.

"Mom, school's great, too. We learned more about the Pilgrims today. I want to talk to both of you about this. We've gotta celebrate America like Americans do."

Morrie flashed his dimples, rattled off details of the history of the Pilgrims, how they inspired the American Thanksgiving holiday. He understood the dire circumstances the new American people faced, pleaded to convince his parents they needed to celebrate Thanksgiving.

Abe and Bella found his innocent passion impossible to resist. When Thanksgiving 1934 arrived, the Cutler family celebrated their first American holiday, complete with a roasted goose, the only bird available at Cutler's Market.

The topic of education dominated the dinner table. Abe and Bella emphasized the importance of school every day. Bella, denied an education when a child, impressed the importance of education on her sons, and grandchildren.

Abe and Bella Cutler

One night, I sat next to Bella at Shabbat dinner while she admonished me to keep up my studies. I got good grades but my girlfriends or the newest toy often distracted me.

She told me in Yiddish, "When your great-aunt Alta and I grew up in Russia, only boys attended school, only to eighth grade. In the early 1900s, girls in the old country stayed home, learned to cook, sew, run a household. Your great-grandmother valued education. Each day, while your great-grandfather worked and Banish attended school, she arranged in secret for a tutor to teach us girls how to read, write, understand basic math."

I never knew foreign cultures forbade girls to attend school. My dad always impressed on me the importance of achievement at school. Bella's story made school far more special, helped me understand why my dad, who admired his mother, praised education.

At school and at Speckart's Drug Store, Morrie learned the reality of power existed in real life, not just in stories.

America's founding, the dangerous pioneer journey to the west, the struggle against tyrants all happened because brave people like George Washington, Thomas Jefferson, Clara

Barton, Daniel Boone chose to do the right thing. The fearless characters sought unknown realms, found new lands, grew empires and inspired Morrie to explore the world. The power of flight meant nothing could stop him from seeing the world for himself. He made lists, researched countries he wanted to see.

Morrie's prodigious success at school led to life lessons at home. His parents often cautioned the eager young boy about his desire to lead his class. His father often told him, "A good man does not brag about himself."

They taught him how Jewish families recognized an honorable goal in living the life of a *mensch*—a man of integrity, discretion.

Although Morrie often pretended to mimic superhero bravado, he developed a humble, gentle spirit, vital characteristics of the mensch he wanted to be when he grew up.

Morrie's early zest for life and aptitude for learning enabled him to find a lesson in everything he read. Besides his school books and the prized American history book his father gifted him, comic books taught him handy skills, like how to use logic to find answers, how to get things done while he remained in the shadows, or how to get what he needed without disturbing anyone else.

Morrie loved to learn American lingo from comic books and his pals. He wanted to fit in with American kids whose parents never spoke Yiddish. He tagged along with his big brother Alex, hung out in the streets, and played American baseball. Together, they loitered outside nearby Busch Stadium, home to the St. Louis Cardinals, hoped to catch an up-close glimpse of the legendary players.

Some of the boys found knotholes in the wooden fence around the field to peek through at the games. Morrie, too short to use the existing knotholes, decided to carve a hole at the perfect level for him to peep through.

"Hey Alex, keep a lookout," he said. He pulled a small dinner knife out of his pocket, scraped wood from the fence at his eye-level.

"Hey Moe, where'd you get the knife? From home? Oooo, you're gonna get it. Better not let Mom catch you," Alex said. He playfully ruffled his little brother's curly hair.

Over the course of the season, the boys who peeped through the holes in the stadium fence earned themselves the nickname The Knothole Gang. In a gesture of goodwill to their devoted fans, stadium employees once let the boys in to watch a game for free.

A dream come true!

The game started. Alex made a beeline for the closest seats to the dugouts, told Morrie to follow suit. They sat closer to the Cardinals team than they ever imagined. These gigantic men, who played a mean game of ball, awed both boys.

Smaller in stature than most of the group, Morrie looked up to the ballplayers when they entered or left the stadium. At times, a generous player stopped to sign autographs for the gaggle of boys, which sent them all into a frenzy of hero-worship. They compared baseball cards, autographs.

"Hey there lads, how's it look on the field?" A deep voice boomed behind the row of boys, their eager faces pressed to their eyeholes.

Morrie spun around from his own personal eyehole, found himself face to thigh with a uniformed Cardinal. He staggered backwards until his back pressed against the fence, looked up into Jimmie Reese's face. Morrie flung his hands up to shield his eyes from the sun, whipped his stack of baseball cards in the direction of the giant who towered over him.

"I'm sor-sorry, Mister. You startled me. Hey, you Jimmie Reese?"

"Yeah kid, you got me."

"Can I call you Jimmie? See these Cardinals cards I traded for? Wanna sign one for me, please, Jimmie?"

Morrie dropped to his knees, scrambled to pick up his cards, pounced on a team card, shoved it into the player's outstretched hand.

"I got 'im to sign a card! Woo hoo! He picked me, boys. How about them apples?" Morris said. The other boys swarmed around him to look at the tidy signature above the team picture.

"You're one lucky s.o.b. Moe. I hope I get the autograph next time." Alex kicked the dirt, once again tousled his kid brother's mess of curls. "Some guys get all the luck, eh?"

He spent his free time either at a game in baseball season or enthralled in his cherished comic books. While he lingered on every page, every drawing, he never bought them. The Great Depression wreaked havoc around him. His parents worked harder than ever to keep the family afloat.

He saw his friends attend school in threadbare hand-me-downs. He also wore his brother's hand-me-downs. Since he saw Alex as one of his idols, Morrie loved to parade around in his brother's old, patched clothes. Many of his classmates went hungry on a regular basis, but because Morrie's family saved enough to purchase their own food market in 1933, the year Morrie turned nine, they always put food on the table.

Abe and Bella gave thanks daily for the bountiful food they ate, remembered that the American Dream they achieved in St.

Louis came too late for their two firstborn sons, who died of starvation in war-torn Russia.

The family of four promised each other to forego luxuries like new furniture, new toys, to save enough money to move out of the cramped stock room of Cutler's Market into a real home.

The move became a reality late in 1934, when Morrie turned ten. Frugal living permitted the family to save enough money to rent a modest house with a separate bathroom, kitchen. They celebrated their improved lot in true Cutler style, humble about their achievements together.

They decided to hire a delivery man to take bags of groceries to loyal customers who possessed no reasonable way to transport more than two full bags of items. Their new hire, an honest, easygoing colored man, Sidney Elliott, endeared himself to the Cutler family. Within weeks, Abe and Bella invited him to stay at their new home. For the ten years he lived there, worked for the family, Sidney drove a dilapidated green truck, "Cutler's Market" painted on the doors.

At break times and on Shabbat, Morrie listened to Sidney tell elaborate stories of his adventures. Sidney shared a lifetime of experience, taught young Morrie manly things like how to drive a stick-shift car or roll a Bull Durham cigarette. Over the years, Morrie realized Sidney's character exemplified the qualities of a mensch. He wanted qualities like this man, who he treated as an uncle.

A few times, Morrie fell short of his goal. The birth of his baby sister, Shirley, opened a sore spot for this otherwise amiable nine-year-old youngster, upset when his parents brought a girl home instead of a boy.

Morrie at 22, Shirley at 13

When his parents explained why people don't get to choose if they have a boy or girl, Morrie decided to run away. Girls terrified him. This one screamed all the time. He found a brown paper sack from the market, dumped in the essentials: pajamas, and his prized possessions, gifted comic books. He slung the crumpled paper bag over his shoulder, headed down the road to Speckart's Drug Store. Unsure what to do, he whiled away the hours in his usual spot at the end of the magazine aisle. Around dinnertime, the rumble in his tummy, the cool chill of the evening convinced him he could learn to endure a sister. Defeated, he trudged home.

Although he had a sister, Morrie remained uncomfortable around girls. He taunted his sister, often kicked her under the table at dinner until she burst into tears, ran to her room, or until his father commanded, "*Zall zein schtill!*" (It should be quiet!) Later, when he neared Junior High School, he attended the local community's Council House, where he developed courage to talk to girls.

The Council House, later renamed The Boys and Girls Clubs of America, became an instant hangout for neighborhood kids. The House organized children into age groups, which picked their own names. Morrie's group chose The Vancors.

A young law student, Ralph Kalish, led them. He taught the boys his "Rules of Order" to enhance their ethics, core values, polite social skills, among them ballroom dance lessons. Morrie signed up to learn how to dance, how to talk to the ever-so-daunting girls. Despite only brief contact with Ralph Kalish, Morrie took Ralph's lessons to heart, relied on the codes of conduct from the Rules of Order classes to help him become the mensch his parents wanted.

In September 1937, Bella, Abe, the entire synagogue congregation celebrated Morrie's bar mitzvah, the rite of passage into manhood. After years of mandatory practice that kept him from his first love, the baseball field, he sang, read from the Torah with the rabbi.

Thirteen-year-old Morrie stretched on his tiptoes to replace the heavy, sacred Torah scrolls back in their proper place on the pulpit, like he stretched for greater achievement in his present and future life.

5

WORLD WAR II

On high alert after his Commanding Officer woke him at 4 a.m., Morrie rushed into a preflight briefing to receive emergency orders for his fourth mission since he graduated Navigation school as a 2nd Lieutenant.

Headquarters notified the squadron of German anti-aircraft artillery installed around the city borders of Munich, which put every flight crew member on this bomber mission at great peril. German soldiers spotted incoming planes fast, fired with pinpoint accuracy. This new mission instilled an unfamiliar, profound fear in Morrie. Munich, deep in German territory, required the team to fly at least ten hours, most of the flight in enemy skies.

Morrie in World War II

The squadron took an hour to prep for the dawn mission. Morrie completed the preflight figures, plotted their course, suited up for the most grueling mission yet. Four hours after takeoff, Morrie confirmed entry into enemy territory, the ten flight crewmembers went through steps to release the bombs above Munich. Morrie, who stood behind the bombardier on previous missions, sat frozen to his desk in the middle of the plane. He read maps, confirmed coordinates, hoped his fellow crew members couldn't sense his fear.

The pilots radioed back to Morrie when they spotted eighty-eight box guns on the ground. Seconds later a barrage of shells hammered the plane. Morrie watched the bombardier, Buffington, get shot out of his seat, thrown far enough into the air to land behind Morrie's chair. Bloodstains spread across the back of Buffington's flight suit. All Morrie's training kicked in. On instinct, he bolted toward Buffington's original post, jettisoned the last of the bombs. The pilots cheered when they exploded on the artillery stations below. Morrie glanced toward the pilots, noticed a bullet hit the radio operator. The plane lost altitude.

Morrie scrambled back to his desk. He called in new flight plans to take them to Switzerland, hoped the crippled plane could fly there. He turned to Buffington, grabbed the first aid kit off the metal wall, reassured his friend he'd survive. Buffington groaned in pain every time Morrie moved him. Morrie administered a shot of morphine, bandaged the wounds, wrapped him in a green Army-issued blanket.

Switzerland, the closest neutral territory, lay seventy miles away. The injured plane descended too fast. The crew discussed the best options to keep the plane aloft long enough to reach friendly soil. They tossed out weight like guns, ammunition, the ball turret. Morrie watched the rest of the squadron disappear north, back to their base in Debach, England. Left on their own, no way to defend themselves, Morrie felt more vulnerable than ever.

On constant watch, Morrie spotted a lake in the distance. He checked his map, informed the pilot, "We drifted north away from Switzerland, fifty miles to the Rhine River. Let's get to the French border."

Alex and Morrie Cutler in uniform in World War II

The plane responded like molasses to the pilots' maneuvers. They realized they needed to make an emergency crash landing, they hoped on friendly soil. The plane dropped to 6,000 feet.

Thirty miles from the three borders of Germany, France, Switzerland, the tail gunner spotted four enemy ME109s lined up in attack formation behind them. Morrie looked around for help. No ammunition, an easy target. He closed his eyes, thoughts of his life flashed before him. Shots rang out, Morrie flinched, expected the bullets to pierce the hull of the plane. He looked out the window, cheered four American P51 Mustangs on a mission to chase down the enemy planes just like in his comic books.

The outmatched enemy fled, the Mustangs gathered to escort the plane. Past the Rhine River, the Mustang formation tipped their wings to say goodbye. The crew later identified this group of planes by their tail marks, discovered their rescuers' identity, the famous Tuskegee Air Group from Italy.

Minutes after they bid their escorts heartfelt thanks, the crew braced for a crash landing on a French airstrip outside of Nancy, headquarters for the 9th Air Force. The pilots exercised minimal control over the plane, hit the runway, jolted, slid. Ground crews rushed to help the frightened flight crew disembark, carried two wounded men to safety. Once the crew cleaned up, ate, the Air Corps placed them on two-day leave, gave them permission to board a train for Paris.

Morrie arrived in Paris early in the morning. The crew made their way to the old St. Francis Hotel, located near Notre Dame Cathedral, where the French treated them like American heroes for their role in their dangerous mission. Despite the dingy accommodations, they relished the clean, comfortable beds, grateful for the company of brothers. Each man settled in, rested, veiled the shared rooms in silence. After flying over ten hours, no sleep for more than twenty-four, the men drifted into slumber, either heavy or anxious.

Morrie closed his eyes, spent most of the day lost in thought, reflected on how he made it to the present, thankful to survive.

He squeaked into aviation officer training, chuckled at his youthful audacity at an intense bickering match with his sergeant the fated morning he took the assessment test to become an aviation cadet. The sergeant didn't let him take the test. Morrie, the brash raw recruit, argued back.

Cutler luck stayed on his side when a captain overheard the argument from his office, strode in to resolve the matter. This seasoned officer respected Morrie, ordered the sergeant to let him take the aviation test. Morrie passed with flying colors, became a cadet, moved toward pilot school, until the final three days of exams revealed poor visual depth perception. His dreams of a fighter pilot career dashed, he went instead to navigator flight training. The years he added columns of numbers on the grocery bags of Cutler's Market customers paid off—he excelled on the navigation examinations, graduated navigation school near the top of his class.

Dad accompanied his new team of graduated navigators to additional preflight gunnery training. At Fort Myers Gunnery School in Florida, Morrie met another young officer, Sol Wynar.

Together these two friends attended advanced flight training at Selma Field, Louisiana. Sol and Morrie relished their wild training adventure. They boarded a B-17 plane, fired two .50-caliber machine guns at numerous aerial targets. This training experience beat playing army back home. Through work and leisure activities, Morrie and Sol's friendship lasted sixty years, until Sol passed away in his mid-eighties.

Lost in the memories of his incredible journey, Morrie dozed off into a peaceful rest, awoke in the early evening ready to enjoy the City of Lights.

Morrie's team made plans to play tourist on their short leave. They visited the typical spots, the Eiffel Tower, the

Louvre, museums, famed architecture. Morrie recalled his extensive reading from schoolbooks, felt the impact when history came to life like he never experienced before. He strolled from the Arc de Triomphe down the Champs Élysées, reflected on the great moments of history these places witnessed.

In the evening, handsome in their American flight suits, the crew returned to the Champs Élysées, sauntered into the cafés along the famed avenue, made their way over to the Moulin Rouge. In a stroke of good fortune, the cabaret opened for one night in honor of a French holiday. The risqué club lived up to the legendary stories Morrie heard over the years. They caroused until the early hours of the morning, cemented an extraordinary friendship. On their way back to the hotel, the men strolled into the night, serenaded the stars, told each other grand stories about the beautiful dame who got away.

Morrie at Debach, England World War II

A few hours after he fell asleep, the sound of fists on his hotel door jarred Morrie awake. His bleary-eyed crew got instructions to catch a train back to the airstrip, where a plane to the base at Debach, England waited for them. When they landed back on base, the staff debriefed the team, released them for a ten-day period of rest, recuperation. Morrie joined several ground officers in recovery from near fatal missions on the front lines. He listened in disbelief to these devastated men tell tales of Jews slaughtered in concentration camps across Europe. Morrie heard estimates of upwards of hundreds of thousands of murdered Jews, recoiled, struggled to make sense of such horrendous violence.

One week later, Morrie returned to his post to fly new missions. Not even the intensity of the missions erased the ground officers shocking conversations. Morrie rehashed the frightening descriptions. Each new mission turned Morrie's attitude darker, more fatalistic. Each mission brought him closer to the Nazi's inhumanity. His anger turned toward God. After a brutal fifteenth mission, Morrie developed a raging desire to destroy the Germans. Disgusted, he questioned a god who allowed such horrific treatment of the Jewish people. These thoughts disturbed him, contradicted his years of study with his rabbi. Morrie felt bewildered by the ravages of war around him, forced himself to put the distressing thoughts out of his head to stay focused, make it through the war alive.

On April 1, the Army Air Corps promoted Morrie to First Lieutenant. Five weeks after his promotion, radios blared the long-hoped-for news of the war's end. Germany surrendered, World War II in Europe ended on May 8, 1945. Installed at Debach Airfield, Morrie kicked up his heels, yelled for joy. His entire squadron smoked cigars, drank champagne, celebrated the nascent European peace through the night.

The fighting around them over, Morrie looked forward to multiple live-saving missions. They flew several more times, returned released prisoners to their homes across Europe.

On their final three days, they dropped food, supplies over villages in Holland to help the starving Dutch. The second time they flew this mission, the crew members felt like superheroes when they took turns at the window to read the heartfelt message the grateful Dutch wrote in large, colorful letters made from tulips: THANK YOU AMERICANS.

Morrie and fellow soldiers at end of World War II in Europe

Morrie stared at the words through a tiny window near the rear of the plane. What a beautiful sight, he thought.

The crew stayed at Debach for a number of weeks to clean up the mess the Germans left, before Morrie got leave to return to the States. They departed Debach on July 2, landed stateside at Logan Field near Boston, Massachusetts July 4, 1945. On arrival on American soil, Morrie treated himself to a quart of milk, two large Tootsie Rolls, the little things he missed while at war. His month of leave back home in St. Louis saw him living life to the fullest. He ate, drank, caroused, blew a thousand dollars. After the utter devastation in Europe, he knew he spent way too much, but, grateful to arrive home alive, he didn't care.

The end of his leave neared when he received new orders to report to duty in Sioux Falls, South Dakota, where the Army Air Corps reassigned him to a new B-29 crew. Morrie celebrated the prospect of flying one of the latest planes with a new crew, but fate intervened to stop his military career.

Days before he reported for duty, America dropped two atomic bombs on Japan, the war ended on all fronts. The Army issued new orders for Morrie to return to Jefferson Barracks in St. Louis. Although Morrie served less than the mandatory three-year term, he received an honorable discharge because of his heroism. Three days before his twenty-first birthday, Morrie accepted his papers, his freedom.

Free to go where he pleased, Morrie took a two-day train ride west to join his family in Los Angeles, where they moved earlier in the year. On the two-day journey, Morrie took time to reflect. The experience of war, the passage of time changed him in innumerable ways. He became sharper than ever before. His experience helped his confidence skyrocket. He stared out the train window at the undeveloped land he passed through, realized he faced his own new frontier. Like a new man, Morrie controlled his destiny, able to accomplish whatever he set his mind on. Morrie nodded in acknowledgement of the unlimited potential of his future, cast his next challenge: graduate from college.

6

SCHOLARLY LOVE

Morrie guzzled the sweet lemon-lime fizz of Bubble Up. Why did I come here, he thought? He regretted giving up his butcher's apprentice shift to hang out at this Hollywood house party with his friend Tim. He needed the money.

Morrie glanced across the room, over the green Bubble Up bottle tilted like a pirate's spyglass toward the door. Lost in his thoughts about girls, work, his classes at UCLA, he stopped bobbing to the beat of Benny Goodman's big band orchestra. Tamara, the attractive young hostess, swished by him.

The front door opened. Morrie froze. A radiant full moon against the velvet blackness of the October sky created an ethereal sight, a stunning backlit young woman. She glided across the threshold, gave the beautiful hostess an affectionate peck on the cheek.

In that enchanted moment, Morrie's heart thumped in time to the music. The girl dazzled him brighter than a Hollywood movie star, struck him like a lightning bolt. Her silky black hair hung in two sleek chignons above the nape of her neck. Her blue eyes glittered in the evening lights, her ruby red smile outshone the chandelier above her. Around her neck, a long strand of pearls cascaded down the front of her floral print dress, refined, sophisticated, hugged her voluptuous figure in all the right places.

Morrie in college at UCLA

"Va va voom!" Morrie thought. He watched the vision make her way further into the room.

"Everyone, I'd like to introduce my sister, Faye, her date Tom," Tamara said. She hugged her sister from the side.

Morrie took another swig of Bubble Up, never released his eyes from this lass lovelier than any woman he'd ever seen, didn't notice the gentleman beside her. It didn't take long for the orchestra's playful beat to persuade partygoers to make their way to the makeshift dance floor. Faye's date said a few words to her, left the party. She closed the front door behind him, rejoined the party, swayed in time to the rhythm, giggled. Morrie decided to make his move.

"It's about time you got rid of the guy you brought," he said.

Lucky for Morrie, Faye smiled. "I came home early because my date bored me. My sister's party had to be more fun."

Morrie hoped he sounded intelligent enough to impress this woman. He talked about how the Federal government's GI Bill funded his college education, how the Enrollment Registrar at UCLA awarded him 38 units for his military officer training. Conversation with Faye felt easy. Words flowed out of his mouth like a water faucet. "I want to teach high school English and History, create a positive difference for young people," he said. He noticed the pearls caught in her deep cleavage.

Faye thought him mature from his experience in the war in Europe. Minutes passed, the two shared school stories, aspirations until Tamara swept Faye away. She said, "I need to introduce my sister around."

Disappointed the magical moment ended, Morrie ambled over to his friend, Tim.

"You know she's jailbait, right?"

"What do you mean?" Morrie asked.

"She's Tamara's *younger* sister. She's in high school, buddy."

"So, she's a senior?" Morrie asked.

"No way man, she's only fifteen."

"What? You've gotta be kidding." Morrie wondered how to navigate this new problem.

The next Sunday, Tamara brought Faye to the ballpark. Several of her friends played on Morrie's softball team. Morrie guarded second base, thrilled to see Faye in the stands. She wore her silken black hair down, which made her far more captivating. After the game, Morrie verified Faye's age, only fifteen years old. He reached into his front pants pocket, pulled out a nickel, the price of a phone call back then, flipped a nickel toward Faye, said, "Honey, call me when you turn eighteen. I'd love to take you out."

Faye reached out, caught the nickel! She held up the shiny silver coin, lowered her dark lashes, flashed her radiant Hollywood smile, countered Morrie's flirt with silence.

Faye's innocent charm guaranteed Morrie saw her far sooner than three years, not even three months! The next week, he asked for permission to take her on their first date, a visit to a traveling circus. Smitten, each by the other, their one date turned into many, set off a lifelong romance.

Morrie held doors open for Faye, pulled out her chair at cafes. The dance lessons he took at Council House paid off. He loved Faye's bright enthusiasm when he asked for her opinion on his career goals. In high school herself, Faye admired his intelligence, ability to earn all "A"s. Morrie attended classes, studied, typed papers, worked fulltime as a butcher. Faye cheered him on when he graduated with honors in two years, earned two bachelor's degrees in English and History in 1948.

The summer of 1949, while enrolled in graduate school at USC, Dad experienced an epiphany: The fundamental strategies basic to his academic learning theory.

Morrie with his softball team, front, second from left

Sprawled on the living room sofa, his leg propped on a pillow from a softball injury, an ice pack draped across his ankle, he read a book called *The Foundations of Reading*.

Mid-afternoon, he saw it, there on the page, the answer: "When students learn to read, comprehend, apply concepts, they unlock the door to all learning." What a huge revelation! Any reservations Morrie felt about his future goals vanished, his life purpose in education became clear. This eye-opening vision showed him the true value of education. Much like the story of Ali Baba, who stood in front of the cave, he uttered "Open Sesame." In an instant "the jewels of education" lay at his feet.

My father realized reading cultivated young minds, provided tools to harvest information for thinking, creativity, solving problems. Educators used this data to fertilize theories, test the principles, and evaluate them. Shazam! The answers appeared. A wide-open path unfolded, the journey to his future looked crystal clear.

Morrie the groom

Another fact, the way he and Mom felt about each other. Morrie bequeathed his unconditional love to Faye on August 27th, 1949, two months after she graduated from Fairfax High School. The two exchanged marriage vows, began to paint the portrait of their lives together.

Wedding party

Morrie and Faye's wedding 1949

7

FAMILY BEGINNINGS

Morrie stood on top of the world with his stunning bride. He reflected on how much he overcame, his strong confidence, how this former Air Corps Officer tackled obstacles. He looked forward to all they'd accomplish together.

Morrie and Faye whispered late into the night about their hopes to start a family, for Morrie's success in education, for their desire to travel to exotic lands. Morrie recounted to Faye the years his family scrimped to save up for Cutler's Market. They committed themselves to the same course, live a simple life, no luxuries. Their future life, and family reaped the dividends.

They wanted a tight-knit family, did everything to ensure the family's success. Those around my parents witnessed a couple who loved each other. Morrie and Faye worked hard to build their future.

Morrie's enthusiasm, work ethic, supportive wife helped him sustain the energy he needed to work his full-time position as teacher of remedial reading at Wonderland Elementary, and his two part-time jobs while he finished his master's degree at USC. Faye became a bookkeeper for RCA, the electronics company, while Morrie brought home the bacon from his after school, part-time butcher job. They moved into a 400-square-foot bungalow, where he could use the toilet and eat dinner at the same time. They furnished their home the same way as the young immigrant Cutler family, with mismatched, worn hand-me-down pieces and made the place work. Faye used a large bed sheet to cover the wear on the sofa. Morrie used a book of matches to even the legs of the donated dining room table.

These early years of make-do bonded my parents in a loving relationship, saw them through decades of highs and lows together. Morrie took a giant leap forward in June of 1951, when he finished his master's degree in Education Administration. His epiphany about how to improve students' learning outcomes by improving their reading skills provided a vivid view of his future career path.

Then everything changed.

Faye came home from the doctor one night. "I'm pregnant," she said.

For the past three years they'd lived in the tiny bungalow they rented from my grandmother Jenny, Faye's mom. But Morrie knew they needed to buy a family home. Over the next few months they viewed homes, crunched numbers, updated their plans. In 1952, Jenny gave them a generous loan, qualified them for a GI mortgage loan.

Three weeks before the baby was born, as most new mothers did, Mom left her bookkeeping job.

A week after they moved into their first home on Greenbush Street in the San Fernando Valley, their daughter, Terri, made her anticipated arrival. My elated parents watched their dreams come true. Their brand-new, affordable three-bedroom, one-bath home in a new family community became the perfect place for their family to grow. My dad already saw the enhancements he wanted to make to give us kids places to play. Morrie loved to return home to his loving wife, giggling daughter, who shared his same curly hair, dimpled chin. He proclaimed it the greatest moment of his days, aside from his professional accomplishments.

Morrie, committed to make learning easier for students, wrote his own textbook in a second-grade vocabulary. *An Early History of the United States,* a pivotal text in his classrooms, helped students overcome reading difficulties and learn research skills.

Though never published, he made several copies of the text. The detailed stories of American history impressed me more than the fact that he wrote the book. He combined many aspects of the items he loved into the textbook—comic book storytelling, American heroes and events, reading comprehension, a joy of learning. He infused life into the text to make early American history simple for students.

Over the course of 1953, life flowed along, followed my parents' plans. Morrie kept busy at work. On weekends he spent family time with Faye and Terri or worked on home improvement projects with his close friend, Baxter.

He felt like their work paid off, thought life couldn't be sweeter—until Faye announced her second pregnancy. My again elated parents fixed up space for the new baby. Her pregnancy progressed, Morrie and Faye's grateful joy increased. Within a few months of the start of her pregnancy, Faye miscarried. My parents dropped into deep sadness, worried they'd never realize their dreams of a big family. They consulted with doctors, received permission to try again. Soon thereafter, my mom became pregnant for the third time.

On October 2, 1954, two years after Terri's arrival, my brother, Wayne, entered the world. My father's dreams to play baseball, read comic books with a son became a distinct possibility. To add to the joy of Wayne's arrival, my parents celebrated when their close friend Baxter agreed to become Wayne's godfather.

Both Morrie and Faye kept busy for the next year. In May 1955, Morrie changed schools to teach 6th grade at Haddon Elementary. Faye took care of two young children while she ran the household.

In June, he received a letter from the US Air Force, an invitation to attend an exclusive meeting. At the meeting, Dad learned the Rand Corporation completed a study after the Korean War, outlined an urgent need for an emergency military force ready to take action within 8,000 miles of our borders. They established the Civilian Reserve Training Unit. The requirements for reservists included to report for duty one weekend a month, participate in one fifteen-day mission per year to train with the latest navigational equipment. If the government declared a State of Emergency, this force of reservists flew into action to transport troops or supplies anywhere the military needed them.

Dad signed up, thrilled this new challenge gave him an opportunity to serve his country again. Also, the additional income helped him take care of his growing family.

Faye once again announced a pregnancy. Delighted by news of a third child, Morrie worked to increase his earning potential. He studied for, passed the Vice Principal exam. Though grateful for his appointment to a school administrator position at Glenwood Elementary School in the fall of 1955, another miscarriage broke Morrie and Faye's hearts.

Because of complications from the miscarriage, future pregnancy put Faye's health at great risk. Doctors cautioned her against further attempts to conceive another child. However, Faye wanted another. She ignored the recommendation, became pregnant again. On June 5th, 1956 my mother gave birth to her last child, me! The doctors' warning about the health risks of another pregnancy proved accurate; my mom almost died when she gave birth to me. After the delivery, they rushed Mom into emergency surgery, after which she spent three weeks in recovery at the hospital.

The day after my birth, Dad wrapped me up like a pink burrito, took me home. Because Mom needed to stay at the hospital, the doctor sent a pediatric nurse to care for me. Our grandmother, Jenny, took care of Terri and Wayne. Our family appreciated the support running the home front while my mother convalesced. Dad visited Mom daily, spoiled her with flowers, regaled her with stories about Terri and Wayne's funny shenanigans.

8

THE STORYTELLER

Dad loved to tell stories. His tales of historic events always engaged me and strengthened my desire to learn. They ranged from Leif Erickson's discovery of America, Christopher Columbus sailing the ocean blue, to Paul Revere's Midnight Ride through Boston, Massachusetts shouting, "The British are coming!"

His stories at times turned more personal, even mischievous. One sunny spring day, about my third birthday, Dad and I sat on the steps of our front porch on Greenbush Street talking. I don't remember the subject. With a thunderous racket, the garbage truck rumbled up our block, distracted us. Earlier Dad rolled the silver metal trashcans out to the curb with his big red dolly. I don't think he ever knew my brother

Wayne once gave me a ride on the dolly. When he pushed me too fast, I slid off, skinned my knee.

Dad pulled me close. In a serious tone he said, "If you get too close to the trashcans on trash day, the trash men might mistake you for a trashcan, throw you into the big garbage truck, haul you away to the trash dump."

At the age of three, I believed the tales my father told. Nothing happened, but the warning stuck. From then on, whenever I heard the trash truck, I panicked, ran into the house, hid under my bed until the noise faded. A few times, I hid in my closet behind the clothes. This vivid paranoia, silly now, haunted me for years.

Flash forward two years, to my first year of school at the age of five. In 1961, like clockwork Monday through Friday, moms stayed home while dads went to work in the morning, returned home in the evening. Kids played Kick the Can—a version of Hide and Go Seek—in the street. Our lives looked much like the *Ozzie and Harriet Show,* which aired on TV from 1952 to 1964.

My school adventure started when Mom walked my neighbor Bruce and me to kindergarten for a couple of weeks to make sure we knew the way. Then she proclaimed us safe to walk on our own. On a beautiful autumn day a few weeks later, Bruce and I walked ten of the twelve blocks to Beachy Elementary School, stopped along the way to examine a caterpillar, cool rocks, other treasures Mother Nature planted along the way.

When we saw the silver chain link fence around our playground, a low throaty rumble touched my ears. I turned around, my mouth open. A trash truck thundered up the street right at me. Dad's warning flashed into my head. I told Bruce in a panicked voice, "I have to go home. You go to school by yourself, I'm going home."

I ran fast as my little black and white saddle shoes carried me. Dad's words echoed all the way. I ran ten blocks without stopping. Who knows if I looked both ways when I crossed the streets? I went on a mission to hide from the trash men. They couldn't catch me, throw me in the big smelly garbage truck.

The front screen door slammed behind me. Out of breath, I cried at the top of my lungs, "*Mom!*" She left the laundry half folded, ran into the room. Tears rolled down my face. Through a shaky voice, I explained Dad's warning, my plight. I'm sure she chuckled inside, yet Mom in her loving way, calmed me down with a generous dose of hugs, cookies and milk.

I'm embarrassed to admit this horrified fear of trash men lasted until ten years old. Many nightmares later, Dad helped me overcome this ridiculous fear with heartfelt discussions.

He said, "I teased you, never thought you'd take my words literally."

With a chuckle in his voice, Dad gave me a sincere apology for tormenting me with his creative imagination. I long since forgave him.

9

THE GOLDEN AGE

When Dad began his part-time career in the reserves, life took off for the Cutler family. At home, we enjoyed the benefits of the second income, but Dad also delighted in the additional opportunities to grow. He committed to the new Air Force Reserve program as a navigator. His teaching background opened new doors with the program.

The Air Force sent him to Mather Field, outside of Sacramento, to become an instructor. In addition, he found the subject of meteorology fascinating, He enjoyed the way advanced technology improved how we understand weather patterns. When he expressed his interest, he got permission to study meteorology and soon became a subject matter specialist for the reserves.

Dad knew his family missed him during his once-a-month weekend assignments, but he loved the travel opportunities. This rekindled his lifelong love affair with history with a new intensity when he traveled to numerous foreign locales, where he basked in the experiences each new culture bestowed on him.

Dad deployed for two weeks in 1960 to Japan by way of Hawaii, Wake Island. He arrived home loaded down with goodies for the family. I cradled my new, hand-carved, wooden doll. We sat cross-legged on the carpet around him in his cozy armchair while he regaled us with stories of his reservist adventures.

He flew a bone-aching, noisy seventy-two-hour, round-trip flight in a C124 supply plane. On the stop at Wake Island, he meandered around the six-mile atoll to witness the results of World War II for himself. The Japanese controlled the island during the war until American Marines, local civilians, heavy bombing gained it back. Dad described a ruined landscape without trees, shrubs, or plants over two feet tall. Among the remnants of the war: bombed-out military pillboxes, burnt-out tanks, abandoned vehicles, grass shacks, huts. He revealed the scene for us like an early explorer who discovered a primitive island for the first time. Wayne rolled on his back, pointed an imaginary gun at the ceiling, made artillery noises.

In Japan, his pilot and copilot escorted him around Tokyo. He saw sights, learned about the culture of a place he knew little about. He explained the Japanese showed American military members an abundance of respect since they saw the Americans as conquerors. He showed us a Japanese ceremonial bow. We giggled, practiced the deep bow in a sign of respect to our own "Fly Boy."

Dad tried new cuisines, visited historical sites, immersed himself in the foreign culture. On his free-time forays, he played Morrie the man, with no kids, no wife to slow down his explorations.

He made a point in Japan to visit schools, where he made friends with Mary, a charming elderly schoolteacher. They conversed about various educational topics, each shared insights about how to improve education. Mary helped him practice his Japanese while she improved her English. After his second visit to Japan, she insisted he call her Aunt Mary. Each time he returned to Japan, Mary invited him to her family's home for dinner.

Faye with children Terri, Diane, and Wayne

Mom looked forward to the times Dad returned from his Reserve duties. When he left, she took care of the three of us kids alone, although if she had any complaints, she told no one. She often reminded us how Dad's patriotic role helped the country, helped us afford a comfortable lifestyle.

With the second income, Mom and Dad made improvements to the house. Dad created the coolest backyard on the block. Once he completed the patio overhang, he added a climbing rope to build our strength. When the Los Angeles School District banned swings from playgrounds, Dad brought three of them home for us. He hung them on the eves of the patio overhang.

Later, Dad built us a gingerbread playhouse with scalloped edges on the roofline and a blue door. Since more boys than girls lived on our block, the playhouse soon became "the fort." When he heard this new nickname for the playhouse, Dad built a vintage wooden wall in front of the fort five feet high with posts on the inside ledge. He showed us how to climb up, pretend to shoot the enemies who attacked us. Then we played Cowboys and Indians, or picked teams, called our sport Bloody Murder. Sounds gruesome, but made good, clean fun for our group of fifteen neighborhood kids.

Wayne, Morrie, and Diane

Dad, a teacher by trade, made the smallest moments into life lessons. Early one spring, Dad took me to the nursery for a special outing. Mom stayed home with Terri and Wayne while Dad and I picked out new flowers for the garden. Dad gave me permission to pick a pony pack of my own. The flowers' colors delighted me. I grabbed a pack of pansies in full bloom to hand to my dad. "What beautiful pansies," he said.

With great patience, he touched the closed buds on a neighboring pony pack of pansies, explained buds. "If you take home the pansies with blooms, the flowers will die in a few days. However, if you purchase the pansies with the buds, you'll enjoy the rainbow colors of the blooms longer."

Although at age four I wanted the instant gratification of flowers already in bloom, I went along with his suggestion. We took home several pansy packs with unopened buds. In the afternoon we planted the new pansies together. I went out to the garden every day, anticipated the jewel-colored blossoms, cheered when the buds opened in a colorful palette over the next few weeks. From the tender age of four, Dad's lesson about delayed gratification stayed with me my whole life.

10

MEXICO AND BEYOND

In 1964, Uncle Alex took his family on a one-year sabbatical, rented a splendid, hacienda-style, nine-bedroom home in Guadalajara, Mexico. In the spring, after several years of Dad's reservist travels and many grand improvements to our Greenbush Street house, Dad announced, "We're flying to Mexico to visit Uncle Alex and Aunt Ruth this summer!"

My first step outside the United States. In my excitement, I danced my version of *La Cucaracha*. Wayne mimicked me. Terri looked on, rolled her eyes at both of us.

Dad applied for passports, visas while Mom shopped for clothes, suitcases, everything a family of five needed to travel to Mexico. At the dinner table, Dad taught us Spanish words in preparation for our big trip. We three kids packed our individual suitcases.

The final night before we left, Dad came into my room, watched me add clothes to my flowery pink suitcase. He gave me his intense Cutler look, said, "If you bring it, you carry it," then he turned, walked out. Those words still ring in my ears. Since then, packing light became a family tradition.

We arrived at Los Angeles International Airport early. Dad pulled five suitcases out of the car. My suitcase weighed more than I did. I followed my parents, struggled to pull my suitcase through the parking lot, but it toppled over. I stood there, Dad's words from the night before rang in my ears, "If you bring it, you carry it." But Dad turned his head, saw me struggle to right my toppled luggage. Without a word—or the Cutler look—he grabbed my bag's handle, tucked it under one arm. We carried on. In those moments, I basked in my father's love.

After check-in, Dad treated us to frosty root beer floats. While we sipped our sweet drinks, Dad shared his vast knowledge of flight. "You must wear your seatbelts for the entire flight," he said.

With his hand extended flat like an airplane, he showed us how the plane ascends after takeoff, then levels out. He explained what pilots, co-pilots do in flight. Amazed by all the details, I thought my Dad knew everything!

Somewhere on the first leg of the flight, turbulence kicked in, my stomach kicked out the root beer float, my introduction to barf bags on a plane. After I threw up, Dad said, "You look white as a ghost, but you'll survive."

Our magical trip included time in Mazatlan, Guadalajara, Mexico City. At the first stop in Mazatlan, we frolicked in vivid aquamarine waters. Dad, Terri, and Wayne swam out beyond the breakers, I stayed behind with Mom. She held my hand, we watched the three of them bob in the ocean swells. I set a goal to find the confidence to one day swim far out in the deep blue ocean with Dad.

When we made it to Guadalajara three days later, we visited with Uncle Alex, Aunt Ruth, a crowd of cousins. In Tlaquepaque's markets, Dad practiced his Spanish with the shopkeepers. We also swam in an Olympic-sized swimming pool at a country club. One day, we rode horses. One evening, while the adults went to a cocktail party, all nine of us cousins piled into a taxi to see a movie. For the first time, I experienced a movie with English subtitles. Dad later asked if I read fast enough to keep up with the story.

For the last part of our trip, we stayed in a gorgeous high-rise hotel in downtown Mexico City. Dad splurged on separate inexpensive hotel rooms in Mazatlan, Mexico City, to give he and Mom alone time. Dad let us play on the elevators the first day. We rode up and down, pretended to be astronauts in rocket ships, divers in submarines.

Dad took all of us to Teotihuacán to climb the Pyramid of the Sun. On our way up, Wayne ran in front, raced up the hundred tiny, grass-covered steps, beat us all to the top. Wayne loved to take the lead. When we all reached the crest of the pyramid, looked out, Dad told us stories of the ancient Aztecs who lived there. He never sugarcoated his stories or told fairytales about princes who saved princesses.

We huddled close around him, listened to tales of days long ago when Aztec warriors played a barbaric kind of ball game. The heroic winner of the game grabbed a sharpened stone knife, cut out the heart of the loser. We learned the horses we rode in Guadalajara didn't exist in Mexico in the 1st century, not until the Spaniards arrived in the early 1500s. Slaves moved necessities between the Coastal and Central Aztecs until the horses arrived.

We descended the steep, narrow steps of the pyramid. Dad held my tiny hand the whole way.

When we reached the base, we stopped to listen to a local Aztec guide. He held a cactus out to us, explained primitive survival techniques employed by natives who used the plant. When eaten, he told us, it provides both hydration, nutrition. He snapped a point off the cactus. It broke away from the plant with threads attached. This natural needle and thread sutured open wounds, sewed animal skins for clothing. I glanced up at my own storyteller. Dad beamed. When he traveled, he loved to learn the history of each place from local citizens.

Nothing equaled the joy of our glorious summer vacation until we moved to Northridge in 1965, when I began fourth grade. Mom and Dad continued their conservative spending habits, bought a home in a nicer, newer family community.

Our new house, with four bedrooms instead of three, meant I got my own room. I celebrated not sharing a room with my big sister, Terri. The new house came with a swimming pool. All three of us kids learned to swim like playful sea otters.

One month after our move, the district promoted Dad to Principal of Van Ness Elementary School in Hollywood. He drove thirty-five miles each way, never complained because he enjoyed the challenge of leading his own school. Mom taught us to give Dad twenty minutes of private time in the master suite when he arrived home each evening.

She said, "Running a school involved many pressures. These precious twenty minutes alone gave Dad a chance to return his thoughts to his family."

Before dinner, Dad unwound in the living room in his favorite chair, his feet propped up on the ottoman. Mom performed her magic on the delicious meal she cooked in the kitchen. Like bees drawn to honey, the minute he sat down in his easy chair, we gathered around to vie for his attention, waited our turn before we imparted our childish victories of the day. I waited while Terri and Wayne spoke first. When my turn arrived, I felt Dad's attentive focus.

Although we experienced normal sibling rivalries, our family life included an enormous amount of amusement. Mom and Dad taught us above all else, family members care for each other. Like a Kodak camera captures photo moments, my mind collected many happy memories with my family.

The new promotion meant more money to decorate our new home, to spend on extracurricular activities. We lived the American dream.

A few months before my tenth birthday, the dream shattered. The frolicking, the joy, the laughter vanished like a magician's illusion after Mom took Wayne to see our pediatrician. Soon, Dad took off work to join them for multiple visits with Dr. Goldwyn, then to see more specialists. At eleven years old, doctors diagnosed Wayne with a malignant brain tumor. "No cure, rare, not a lot of research." They sent Wayne home with one medication to reduce the danger of seizures. My parents kept our home life normal as possible, but the golden era of the Cutler family lost its luster.

11

THE BLUE PERIOD

Soon after the doctors diagnosed Wayne, Dad dropped out of the doctoral program at BYU extension because he could no longer concentrate. He fulfilled his monthly weekend flying commitments with the Air Force Reserves but though Dad loved flying, he didn't want to leave his family at such a crucial time of need.

Wayne underwent two brain surgeries to prolong his life. Though he endured a great deal of discomfort, he surprised us all, maintained a cheerful attitude. Wayne's adventurous, jovial courage strengthened our spirits.

Dad maintained his stoic exterior, yet on the inside he felt helpless. He wanted to save his son's life but saw no hope.

While this happened, Terri, a boy-crazy early teenager, thought little about her actions. Older than me, she understood Wayne's illness differently than I. Our parents focused most of their time on Wayne. Terri rebelled, part because of her age, part because of the lack of attention at home. She defied boundaries, broke rules. This caused more *tsuris* (aggravation) for Mom and Dad. They had their hands full.

At first, I compared Wayne's illness to measles or chicken pox. I hoped for complete recovery. He never got better. Two weeks prior to his death, Wayne went into a coma. Mom and Dad stepped into my room to tell me, "Wayne will die from his illness. "He passed away June 7, 1968, two days after my twelfth birthday, a dark moment for our family.

After Wayne's death, sadness draped our home like a black veil. Dad became more subdued. The joys of our family life diminished, the sweetness dissolved. It made no sense for Wayne, a charming innocent boy near manhood, to die. No one offered answers, not even Dad.

Again, Morrie asked, "Why does God let this happen?"

The tragedy of his lost son, along with his unanswered questions from WW II, caused him to decide no God existed. He became agnostic in his spiritual beliefs. He saw no reason to believe in God. He kept his thoughts to himself, never forced his views onto Terri or me. He didn't criticize others who accepted God. Morrie created his own future with hard work, clear focus on his goals.

In the months after Wayne's death, Dad turned quiet, distant. Late into the evenings, he sat in his big chair in the corner of the living room, read book after book to escape from reality. I knew not to bother him. No one spoke of Wayne.

12

LIVING ONWARD

Dad grieved, learned to incorporate Wayne's memories into his life. He helped our entire family realize we needed to be present in our grief for Wayne, but not let it define us. To overcome his sorrow, Dad channeled his emotional energy toward helping others. He lived life the way he wanted the world to be. After months of mourning, my father decided he needed a change of environment. Parent-teacher meetings often lasted late into the evening. His long commute kept him away from home too many hours. Dad asked the district for a transfer to a school campus closer to home.

The Superintendent reassigned him to Encino Elementary School, only fifteen minutes from home. Many celebrities' children, grandchildren attended this school, Dad's first in an affluent area. The P.T.A. included prominent business professionals' families. His new position produced an array of positive challenges, work healed him. Life brightened, his work added a sense of satisfaction, filled his empty heart with purpose.

Dad's core curriculum at Encino Elementary proved successful on several levels. A team of dedicated teachers in his Reading and Language Arts programs raised the bar for other schools to model. Most students earned high test scores. District level administrators noticed.

Dad recruited devoted parents to assist in each classroom. In addition, he had an uncanny ability to draw out the best in his loyal teachers. Two exceptional teachers from Encino, Roland Faucher and Elaine DuRoff, say Morrie's brilliant mentorship propelled their successful educational careers.

Encino Elementary students used innovative, fun reading, math, and science programs to become among the highest achievers in the Los Angeles Unified School District, helped Dad build an honorable reputation among Southern California educators.

Dad also founded the San Fernando Valley Reading Conference, an annual event to share teaching ideas with educators. The conference became accredited to fulfill the continuing education requirements for credentialed teachers.

In 1968, when Secretary of Defense Robert McNamara cut the Air Force Reserves budget, Dad became a Lieutenant Colonel in the California Air National Guard, based in Van Nuys, fifteen minutes from home. His flexible school principal schedule allowed him to complete required flight times during the week after he finished his school responsibilities for the day.

Over the next few years, Dad flew runs to Italy, Germany, Spain, England, carried personnel and supplies in a Boeing Stratocruiser. These modern planes flew at 19,000 feet, 220 miles per hour with pressurized cabins for more comfortable flights.

At each destination, Dad took two days off. He loved to play tourist, delve into his love of history and the arts. On one extraordinary occasion, he heard Pope Paul VI speak at the Vatican. "Cutler Luck" worked again. Because the men wore American officer uniforms, the guards invited the crew inside St. Peter's Basilica to hear the Pope, a moving experience for an agnostic Jewish boy from St. Louis, Missouri.

On other trips he toured London, Oxford, Naples, Madrid, Majorca. Dad's reserve squadron made a few long-range trips to Panama in an ancient C47. On one trip, they flew to Brooks AFB in Texas to pick up a reserve team to manage control of the Panama Canal if a major war broke out.

The canal company arranged for the aviators to take a short voyage to Gatun Lake on a small steamboat complete with an open bar and a sumptuous BBQ lunch. This created good relations between both Panamanian and American servicemen.

Dad's friendliness paid off again aboard the ship when he met the Director of Public Relations for the canal. My father mentioned he wanted to take his family on a trip to South America. The Director suggested he include Panama in the itinerary. He handed Dad his card. "Alert me when you arrive in Panama. I'll arrange a first-class tour for you."

13

LIVING WITH PURPOSE

It took about two years after Wayne's death for Dad to feel restored. The gaping hole in his heart mended, he appreciated life in a new way. His insatiable thirst for knowledge catapulted him in new directions. He developed innovative curriculum for elementary students, reignited his passion for living. Mom fed off Dad's positive zeal. Although we all missed Wayne, the tone at our home grew lively once again. Pool parties, games, giggles returned.

In the summer of 1970, Dad planned a month-long trip with Mom and me to Central and South America. Terri's full-time bank teller job made an extended vacation impossible. Our itinerary included visits to Colombia, Peru, Argentina, Brazil, Paraguay, and Panama.

Morrie

We began our journey in Colombia, stayed in a luxurious hotel in the heart of downtown Bogotá. After I checked out the marbled bathroom, I pranced into the room. "There's a fountain next to the toilet!" I said. Dad and Mom burst into laughter. It took a moment for them to regain their composure. "It's a bidet," Dad said. "Used to wash our bottoms."

The next morning, we hopped on a local bus, Dad played tour guide for us. The ride on the rickety old bus to the historic cavernous salt mines in Zipaquirá made more of an impression upon us than the mines.

I saw trouble the minute we boarded the dilapidated bus, found every seat but one filled. Dad insisted Mom sit, then showed me how to hold onto the metal poles to keep my balance. The open windows let in a warm morning breeze.

Morrie

I soon realized the novel nature of this bus ride. The passengers, all ages, dressed in faded, threadbare clothes, many with *huarache* leather sandals over their cracked feet, others barefoot. The chickens, geese, a goat made the ride unusual. The bus looked, smelled, sounded like Old McDonald's Farm with a cluck cluck here, a honk honk there. The stench grew worse when the temperatures rose. I gripped the poles with both hands to stay upright, swayed with every turn, bounced at every bump along the pothole-filled roads.

Dad whispered, "See how privileged Americans are? We experience many unnoticed luxuries, like our own vehicles and comfortable public transportation in America." He smiled at my discomfort. "Back home, libraries, paved roads, fire and police services come from our tax dollars. Often we take these public services for granted."

He helped me realize how travel opens our eyes to the reality of how most people live around the world.

Later in life, my father said, "Because we are blessed with opportunities, we need to help others less fortunate."

My father never acted like *The Ugly American* with a sense of superiority. He assimilated into the culture wherever he traveled. He abided by the rule, "When in Rome, do as the Romans do."

To pass the time on the long bus ride, Dad taught me what the word *ethnocentrism* meant, the belief in the superiority of one's ethnic group or way of life over another. "Not true. All people of every race, every country, every faith, are valuable human beings," he explained.

At our destination, the natural salt mines of Zipaquirá fascinated us, worth the stinky bus ride.

Back in Bogotá, we toured the magnificent *Museo de Oro* (Gold Museum). This museum tells the story of Colombia's rich history through crafted golden artifacts from its indigenous people. Armed guards escorted the three of us with seven other visitors by elevator to the second floor. When the electric double doors opened, we all gasped at the opulence. In the small 10-foot by 10-foot room, behind locked panels of glass, we saw a breathtaking array of intricate centuries-old golden artifacts.

On our last day in Colombia, Dad bought Mom a beautiful emerald ring she enjoys wearing today.

We looked forward to Peru, the gateway to Machu Picchu, the lost city of the Incas, the next stop on our itinerary. On the flight, Dad summarized the story of the city's discovery. In 1911, a Yale History professor, Hiram Bingham, after he visited Inca ruins in Cusco, heard about undiscovered Inca ruins. A young Peruvian boy hiked for hours with him through thick tropical jungle to the ruins of Machu Picchu. Though other explorers visited Machu Picchu, Bingham revealed its magnificence to the world.

Machu Picchu amazed us. The Incas built their refuge on more than one hundred terraces of tropical green landscape at the top of an 8,000-foot-high mountain ridge. Machu Picchu combines the majestic grandeur of the Rocky Mountains with the lush beauty of the Hawaiian Islands.

Dad told us the Incas built the ancient city's high-quality masonry in the fifteenth century with no tools or machinery. Dad helped me climb onto a wild llama grazing along an Andean hillside. Later, back in Cusco, he bought me a handmade, stuffed llama keepsake.

We returned to Cusco the night before July 4, 1970. In preparation, I packed sparklers in my suitcase to celebrate our American holiday in Peru. To light pyrotechnics in a foreign country excited us. When we walked down the red-carpeted stairs toward the outdoor patio with sparklers in hand, my mind flashed back to our first day in Peru.

The taxi driver who took us from the airport to our hotel drove past the stately Presidential Palace. He pointed out bullet holes in the white marbled walls. In broken English, he said, "The day before our arrival in Lima, an attempted *coup d' etat* killed many soldiers." We saw a strong military presence, soldiers carried automatic weapons to protect the building's dignitaries.

Dad said to Mom and me, "Now you know why in America we hold democratic elections, to avoid bloody *coups d' etat.*"

Our sparklers made a spectacle for many of the hotel guests, staff. I reflected on the past week with Dad. Profound pride warmed my heart when I recognized our fortunate American citizen status. People marveled at how our glittering wands made circles, zigzags. For Dad and me, waving the sparkling light sticks through the chilly mountain air symbolized America, democracy, and our abundant freedoms.

At our next stop, Buenos Aires, Argentina, Dad took us on a tour of this chic metropolitan city. Beautiful leather shops adorned each street, one swankier than the next. At two o'clock every afternoon, all shops closed for *siesta,* families gathered for a light meal, relaxation. Dad embraced this lifestyle, because he loved to take power naps in the afternoon. We dined every night at ten, early birds for dinner! One evening, Dad ordered a platter of mixed grilled meats. They served us cow testicles with our *papas fritas* (fried potatoes).

In Paraguay, we soaked up the beauty of Iguaçu Falls, the largest in the world. Dad unfolded the map on our flight into Asunción, pointed out the trio of borders Iguaçu touched, Brazil, Argentina, and Paraguay. Dad led us on a tour under, around, over hundreds of cascading falls, through breathtaking scenery. Though we left soaked, the fun hike exhilarated us.

From there, we landed in the exotic city of Rio de Janeiro, Brazil, where we strolled on the artisan-laid, mosaic-tiled

Copacabana Beach boardwalk, licked our icy-sweet cones against a picture-perfect beach backdrop. Under a glorious blue sky brightened by the southern sun, Mom and Dad held hands, marveled at the local handicrafts in the tiny shops. We sensed a renewed wave of happiness.

Iguacu Falls on border of Brazil, Paraguay, and Argentina

Early the next day, we took a taxi to see the famous *Cristo Rendentor* (Christ the Redeemer) on the Peak of Corcovado Mountain overlooking the historic coastline. The 130-foot-high, 98-foot-wide statue, a symbol of Christianity, draws followers from around the world who come to pray, pay homage. Below the statue, the faithful placed gifts. Scores of people walked in a counter-clockwise direction, prayed, asked God for forgiveness. All ages, nationalities, socio-economic levels participated. Many walked for hours around the huge concrete quad, some with swollen eyes, tear-stained cheeks. Several crawled on their hands and knees, blood stained their worn extremities. I didn't understand why people inflicted pain on themselves on purpose. Dad thought after they confessed their sins, this self-sacrificial act exonerated them of guilt.

We enjoyed lunch with local fresh fruits and vegetables, rode a sky tram across the Guanabara Bay to Sugarloaf Mountain. Moviemakers frequent this prime film location because of its splendid view of the Brazilian coastline. Dad loved James Bond movies. "The studio filmed *Moonraker*, with Roger Moore, here," he said.

Next, we stopped in Brasilia, the capital city of Brazil, a sleek, international metropolis. My father wanted to see this planned city filled with modern architecture and more than 100 foreign embassies. Brazil began to plan the futuristic look the year of my birth. Although the city's architecture fascinated us, Dad felt it lacked charm.

We proceeded to Panama for our much-awaited tour of the canal. Before we landed, Dad said, "Prior to the canal's construction in 1914, ships traveling from the Atlantic Ocean to the Pacific weathered the long, treacherous voyage around Cape Horn at the tip of South America."

He pointed out the route on a map. Teddy Roosevelt, one of Dad's favorite presidents, built the most difficult engineering project of the time, the Panama Canal, which cut travel time for ships in half, promoted international commerce.

The director, delighted to see Dad again, treated us like VIPs, guided our tour of the legendary canal in person. He led us through guarded gates where ships waited in line for their turn to pass through the Canal. The Director explained the engineers developed the mechanism to make Panama Canal operations simple.

Gatun Lake, the largest man-made lake in the world, supplies the millions of gallons of water needed to raise and lower each ship when it sails through the canal's three locks. Gravity flow supplied the water to fill each lock. The process took two hours for each ship to pass.

We walked single-file on the narrow locks, followed the director to a tiny booth, the control tower. He said only heads of state and dignitaries get invited onto the locks, into the control tower. I felt proud of my father, who arranged this extraordinary tour for us.

The director pointed out maps, electronic boards, and the large gold lever the managing engineer used to open and close the locks. On impulse, I reached out, grabbed the gold lever. Dad tensed. The director freaked out, lurched forward to remove my hand. I assured them I didn't intend to pull the lever. I wanted to see what it felt like to hold the sleek polished lever like a dignitary.

Our Latin American vacation mended Dad's soul, added a spring in his step. Upon our return home, he acted stronger, more focused. His compass turned, and his adventurous nature ripened again.

Toward the end of his time in the Air National Guard, Dad flew five missions to Vietnam via Guam, the Philippines, Okinawa. Increased combat in Vietnam led to more American casualties. These missions flew additional supplies to soldiers, transported wounded and dead soldiers back home. Mom seemed on edge when Dad flew these tense missions, yet his crew always made a safe return home.

Though our home in Northridge did not lie below any official flight path for commercial or military trips, Dad convinced the pilot to fly over the house before he landed at Van Nuys Air Base. We knew the general time of day to listen for the plane. When I heard the roar, I loved to run out on the lawn to wave my arms, jump up and down. Dad said he saw me. Mom then grabbed her purse, keys. We headed to the landing field to pick him up. We got excited when Dad came home, because he always arrived with gifts.

In 1972, at the age of forty-seven, Dad retired from the Air National Guard as a Lieutenant Colonel. He served his country well, aided his family. His military experience gave him great self-esteem, made him a proud man.

In April 1973, Dad accepted a temporary position with the Los Angeles Board of Education. State legislation required all primary grades (K-3) in California to adopt specific standards. The district hired him to develop then administer the program modifications. He made several trips to Sacramento, met with the State Director of Elementary Education. Dad never grumbled about the forty-mile drive each way to his new office in downtown Los Angeles, because, again, he loved the challenge his work gave him.

After four months of intense effort, he completed the new program. The state held two statewide conferences, one for all district superintendents, a larger one for primary lead teachers and/or principals from each district. They set up two demonstration schools, whose exceptional early childhood programs proved effective.

The assignment offered an accelerated use of Dad's knowledge, experience, and good sense. He considered this a huge honor, although he remained modest about his work.

14

OUR BIG MOVE

Five years after Wayne's death, Dad functioned well—on the surface. He seemed content, yet inside he struggled every day, grieved the loss of his only son. At sixteen, I never saw my father's emotions, because he always appeared in control.

"Let's apply for jobs overseas," he said. "The change will broaden our horizons, create new family memories."

Two years earlier, Uncle Alex and Aunt Ruth moved to Afghanistan to work with the United States Agency for International Development (USAID). In a letter to Dad, Uncle Alex told him the Curriculum Specialist on the educational team ended his contract because he found the primitive environment intolerable for his wife. This job, an opportunity to create a reading program to influence an entire country of students, fit Dad's needs. Uncle Alex submitted Dad's name for the position.

By 1973, Dad's reputation reached beyond California. Richard Whitmore, the Director of the USAID project, appealed to Dad to accept the position. Teacher's College at Columbia University in New York, which supplied most of the members of Richard's Afghanistan team, already knew about my father's dynamic learning programs for early childhood elementary students.

Richard felt pressure from administrative colleagues to hire in house, rather than recruit from outside the team at Columbia University. Richard gave my Dad a huge compliment when he called him the perfect choice.

Richard also explained the importance of family adjustment to the cultural way of life in Kabul, and requested Mom to accompany Dad on his interview to New York. When Dad told me about their upcoming trip, I said, "Don't they want to interview *me*? What am I, chopped liver?" Dad recognized the sarcastic humor I learned from him.

While in New York, Mom and Dad took in the Statue of Liberty, Fifth Avenue, the Empire State Building, a Broadway show, all of which they loved. Of course, they refused to leave New York without eating a hot corned beef sandwich from Katz Deli. They lived life with gusto again.

After New York, when Dad told friends and family about his new job, the reaction was, "You're moving to *Afghanistan*?" In 1973, few knew about the poor, tribal-run nation of Afghanistan.

Dad prepared for his new position, read every available book or article on the people, culture, history, and politics of Afghanistan. He soon became an expert.

At the dinner table, Mom and I heard about Marco Polo, who in the 13th century became one of the first Europeans to reach China. He carried an inscribed golden tablet from Emperor Kublai Khan to ensure safe passage, returned to his Venetian homeland twenty-four years later. Sewn into the lining of his worn garments, he carried exotic spices, exquisite jewels. From Afghanistan he brought treasured royal blue lapis lazuli gemstones. To learn about the jewels excited Mom and me.

Over a thousand years before Marco Polo, Alexander the Great conquered Bactria (ancient Afghanistan) after he defeated Darius III in Persia. Many other rulers of the past swept through the territory, among them Genghis Khan. Dad said, "Although Genghis Khan used brutal, barbaric methods of conquest, killed forty million people, he also adopted a formalized script used in the Mongol Empire."

After World War II, the fear of Communism spread around the world. In 1946, our U.S. Ambassador to the U.S.S.R., George Kennan, wrote a famous twelve-page memo, the "Long Telegram," to the State Department, to show how to halt the advance of Communism. One profound idea: Develop a program to teach English to all high school students around the world. Under Kennan's theory, when younger generations learned English, they also absorbed Western democratic idealism. President Dwight Eisenhower made education an important focus of his foreign policy. Columbia University won many of the educational contracts from the State Department to implement English classes in developing nations.

The British invaded Afghanistan twice in the nineteenth century to protect their lifeline to India. Because of Afghanistan's primitive status, the British invaders wanted to make significant political advances in the country. However, in 1939, the Afghan ruler chose religious tradition and autocratic power over modernization. This caused the people of Afghanistan to stagnate. In the second half of the twentieth century, modern life passed them by.

In 1964, nine years before Dad moved us to Kabul, the United States gave one million dollars' worth of wheat to the Afghan government. This generous donation allowed Afghanistan to sell wheat to the U.S.S.R. to keep their open trade with the communist giant to the north. The proceeds from the wheat sale funded the construction of five schools in cities around Afghanistan, including Kabul University. Before this time, no formal education existed.

For twenty years, the United States provided Afghanistan with assistance in education, agriculture, and infrastructure. Afghanistan soon became an optimistic example of the educational focus in U.S. foreign policy at work. Dad became an intrinsic part of the development.

A primitive, land-locked country, Afghanistan lies high in the Hindu Kush Mountains at the southwestern tip of the Himalayas.

United States Embassy officials warned Americans not to travel by car to the Wakhan Corridor, a narrow area in the far northeast that looks like E.T.'s finger because Chinese bandits hung out there. Despite warnings, curious foreigners who ventured to this beautifully rugged area disappeared. No permanent structures existed for shelter; no drinking water existed during dust-filled droughts in this vast, mountainous desert. *Yurts,* transportable dwellings made of animal skins, uprootable like a tent, gave shelter to bandits on the run. *Kuchis,* a Near Eastern nomadic tribe, often migrated across various borders into this region. Today, studios film movies there, among them *The Kite Runner* and Academy Award winner *Crouching Tiger, Hidden Dragon*.

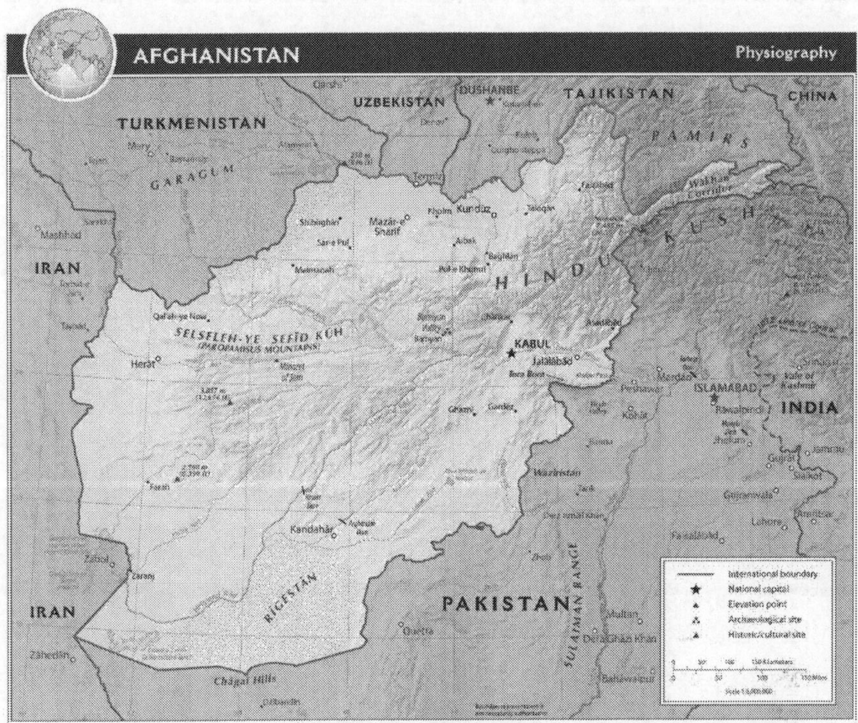

Prior to our departure, Dad received a call from USAID to expect a visit from two men from the Afghan Ministry of Education. Their goals: meet Dad and visit American schools. One of the two men, Haji Tarin, later became my father's revered colleague and friend.

During their stay, Dad arranged tours of several key schools, introduced the Afghan educational writers to American teaching methods. They observed innovative teachers implement new techniques in education. Students' eager interaction added to the lessons. The Afghans studied how students utilized various learning centers in corners of the classrooms, which promoted independence, responsibility, self-discovery, mastery of learning, novel ideas in 1973. Quad cubicles in each corner allowed 16 students at a time to select topics to read based on a variety of interests. Mastery level learning helped measure comprehension, retention. Students also learned accountability, personal responsibility, and to wait their turn.

In addition, Dad contacted Walt Disney's daughter, Diane Miller, a parent at Encino Elementary School, asked her for complimentary tickets to Disneyland for our Afghan visitors. She provided tickets for all of us, arranged for a guided tour of the park.

We enjoyed the wonders of Disneyland through the eyes of two awe-struck Afghan men. Haji Tarin enjoyed the Pirates of the Caribbean, came out excited, exclaimed the *djinns* (ghosts) didn't frighten him. Dad later told me he thought the ghosts scared both gentlemen on the ride but they refused to admit it.

The men asked Dad if Disneyland allowed them to pray. Dad didn't see why not. At the end of Main Street, in front of Sleeping Beauty's Castle, they rolled out tiny prayer rugs hidden in their jackets. They faced east, prayed to Allah. My father thought about Walt Disney, whose goal, to bring people of the world together in this magical place, make their dreams come true, made this a captivating moment.

The men appreciated Mom and Dad's suggestion to cancel their motel room reservations and stay with us during their time in Los Angeles. Dad later learned this saved them per diem money, which they needed for their families in Kabul. This generous gesture made Dad popular in September, when he met the project team in Kabul.

We packed up our home in Northridge. Dad rented it to a new professor at California State University Northridge, a mile from our home. We stored our furniture, large appliances, nicer household items of crystal, china, silver, childhood keepsakes. We shipped our clothing, personal items, all other household essentials to our new home in Kabul. Because this primitive country lacked modern amenities, we needed to bring every household and personal item we'd use for the next two years. No department stores existed to buy underwear or shoes nor drugstores to purchase skincare, shaving cream, or feminine hygiene.

Several months earlier, Terri moved to her own apartment, continued to work for a prominent bank. Mom and I decided to travel to Europe for two weeks. We planned to meet Dad in Istanbul, Turkey, and arrive as a family in Kabul. Dad reported to Washington, D.C. for his orientation with the State Department.

The orientation acquainted Dad with State Department, USAID rules. He appreciated the generous benefits that included my private school tuition, housing, furnishings, and paid vacations every ninety days. The department encouraged vacations in more metropolitan cities in nearby countries to avoid culture shock, keep us assimilated with mainstream life. The State Department did not add to Dad's extensive research, nor did they offer language training, which he thought shortsighted.

Because of the CIA's interest in this region, a CIA official also met with my father. For eight hours, they discussed security for our country, and introduced him to Foreign Service personnel in the region. Until they met, Dad knew nothing of the vast number of people the CIA employed throughout the world.

While the agency briefed Dad for his new assignment, Mom and I loved Europe. Two girlfriends traipsed our way through Portugal, Spain, Italy. We visited historic art museums, basked on gorgeous beaches, ate delicious cuisine, enjoyed the nightlife everywhere. We knew Dad, Terri, and Wayne longed to join us.

After Dad's two-week indoctrination, he arrived in Istanbul with twenty pounds of New York City kosher salami, tired but glad to reunite with his family. We spent two days on the Bosporus Strait, which divides Europe from Asia. This ancient city mesmerized us. Like a magic carpet ride, we explored bazaars more than 2,000 years old and ate the best *baklava* (pastry) we ever tasted.

On our last evening in Istanbul, we boarded a plane for Kabul, our home for the next two years. While Mom and I slept through the flight, Dad closed his eyes, considered the unfamiliar challenges his new position presented, a transition from education administration in Los Angeles to develop a unique language arts curriculum in a Muslim country. His goals for education expanded to a global scale, his thoughts saw the potential of his new assignment, to advance education for an entire nation of children for generations to come.

15

WE'RE NOT IN KANSAS ANYMORE

Uncle Alex, Aunt Ruth, and Dad's writing team gave us a heartwarming welcome at the Kabul airport the morning of September 3, 1973. We felt like celebrities. After we retrieved our luggage from customs, we squeezed into my aunt and uncle's white Toyota Corolla.

Outside the airport, the reality of our move didn't hit me until I spotted the herd of camels on the roadside. Then we passed karakul sheep with wiggly, puffy bottoms that looked like popcorn. Sharp mountains rose up like a circle of brown stalagmites around the city. No longer in California for sure.

Reminded me of Dorothy in *The Wizard of Oz*, "We're not in Kansas anymore."

Dad expected Afghanistan to be a wild, untamed land with high snow-capped mountains, limited rainfall. Although numerous historic invaders crossed these lands, the country remained untouched by the modern world.

The car ride became a family reunion. We chatted, caught up on family news. Dad, who studied a map of Kabul, gazed out the window, said, "We're near Shari Nao, the new city."

In the center of Kabul, Uncle Alex pointed to the tallest building, the Ministry of Education, Dad's office. A mere four stories high, not the Empire State Building, I thought. Aunt Ruth said, "We'll return to Chicken Bazaar to shop later." Dad smiled at Mom and me, since he knew how much we loved to shop.

Our temporary two-story home in Kārta Seh, one of four main sections of the city, included bedding, dishes, cookware, a few staples in the refrigerator, compliments of USAID. The Toyota Corolla Dad preordered waited in the driveway inside the tall, cement walls around our new home. The walls reflected the culture rather than security. A *chowkidar* (gatekeeper), answered the gate night and day, washed the car daily, managed the landscape. We also hired a cook/houseman, Khan Mohammad. We unpacked our luggage, ate a snack, headed for Chicken Bazaar.

Chicken Bazaar sits on the river's edge, though it's not what we'd consider riverfront property. The Kabul River flowed in a cement aqueduct through the capital. On many streets, stairs offered access to the river. Afghans used this water supply for drinking, washing clothes, bathing, defecating. Smelled like it, too.

Dad said, "Drink only designated bottled water, otherwise you might become ill with dysentery."

The American Embassy hosted a fresh-water well. Twice a week, Mom drove to the Embassy to fill two 20-gallon handcrafted metal water jugs. The spout near the bottom of each large jug made filling small containers a breeze. We used this water in small amounts to brush our teeth, soak fruits, vegetables in an iodine solution, drink, make ice cubes.

We walked into our first shop on Chicken Bazaar, a basket shop no bigger than a walk-in closet. Aunt Ruth said we needed to purchase a couple of baskets to carry groceries, other treasures from the bazaar. In Dari, she said to the shopkeeper, "This is their first day in Afghanistan."

He flashed a wide smile, made me feel Afghans, in general, rank among the most hospitable people in the world. We examined a few different sized baskets. Mom picked out two soft, hand-woven baskets with sturdy handles. All the while, Dad practiced his limited Dari with the shopkeeper.

Then the enthusiastic owner handed me a small pink basket with a matching lid, said, "*Baksheesh, baksheesh.*" Because my parents and my aunt accompanied me, I didn't want to ask whether I should smoke it or open it. Dad smiled. "*Baksheesh* means gift," he said. I took the box. Aunt Ruth said to accept his gift made us friends forever. To this day, I treasure the little pink basket, which symbolizes the warm people we encountered in our brief stay in their country.

We left the basket shop. I asked Aunt Ruth, "Why do they call this Chicken Bazaar?"

She said, "I'll show you."

We followed her down the ruddy sidewalk, did our best to not slip into the open *juee,* gutters filled with river water. We passed several Afghan men squatted over the *juee* in their *shalwars* (long shirts). Dad and Uncle Alex later said those men relieved themselves in the *juee*, which pollutes the water.

Three steps further, we passed *naan* (bread) baking in dirt ovens. The fresh aroma made my mouth water. Kabobs cooked on open, hand-made grills, smelled like sizzling beef, although Aunt Ruth said, "Old camel meat."

Dad said, "That sounds appetizing."

Fifty yards along, we found out why they named the street Chicken Bazaar. Hundreds of dead chickens, the heads intact, hung on wooden poles. Flies swarmed everywhere, we batted them from our faces. For the first time I saw dead chickens not cleaned or packaged for sale in a grocery store. Dad said it reminded him of his college days, when he worked as a butcher. I told him. "I think it's gross."

Aunt Ruth purchased two chickens for her cook to prepare for our family dinner. The shopkeeper wrapped them in thin brown paper. My aunt stuffed the package of raw chickens with heads on them into her woven shopping bag.

We walked another block down the river to the Fruit and Vegetable Bazaar. Aunt Ruth called this street Green Door Bazaar, an obvious name. Every tiny shop featured a rustic wooden door painted a version of green. Most of the doors, small, hobbit size to save on lumber, forced me to duck under the doorframes. Fifteen or twenty shopkeepers, the closest thing to a general store, including Indian entrepreneurs, ran shops on Green Door Bazaar. They carried pre-owned household items, used kitchen gadgets, pots, pans, a few imported items from Pakistan or India.

Dad talked with the shopkeepers, practiced Dari he learned from books. My father always created a good example for me when we traveled. He said when we learn the language of the country, we demonstrate respect for people and our willingness to assimilate with them.

Later, Mom and Dad enrolled me in the American International School of Kabul (AISK), located on Darul Aman Avenue. The superintendent, Dr. Gist, said my transcripts showed I didn't have enough credits to meet their graduation standards, much higher than my high school back home. After a short discussion, Dad convinced Dr. Gist to allow me to do independent study classes with the teachers to make up the missing credits. I appreciated Dad, who stood up for me, made my graduation process easier.

We ate a scrumptious chicken dinner. Dad and Uncle Alex talked about their work, politics, the overall economy, the way of life in Afghanistan. Dad looked forward to adventures in the months ahead.

16

WORKING IN AFGHANISTAN

In Afghanistan, Dad developed, wrote a series of formalized reading textbooks for grades one through six, which the Afghan government planned to use throughout the country. His team of Afghan educators translated the reading books into two main languages, Dari and Pashtu. All children, including girls, used the books through sixth grade. Beyond sixth grade, only children whose families with money for tuition received higher education. Haji Tarin, who months earlier visited Dad to observe American teachers in Los Angeles, headed the Afghan team of educators.

A portion of Dad's work included visits to schools throughout the Islamic nation. He took his first business trip on September 24 to Kandahar, the second largest city in Afghanistan, to evaluate a pilot program to implement the first and second grade books developed by the former curriculum specialist team.

Kandahar, a four-hour drive each way, made for a long day. Unsure of protocol, Dad asked Khan, our cook, to pack him a sack lunch for the trip. Dad feared he'd get sick from the street food because in Kandahar food was only available in the bazaars, No Big Macs along the desolate highway below the majestic Hindu Kush Mountains.

Early morning darkness reigned when my father devoured a hearty breakfast prepared by Khan. He stored the sack of food in his briefcase, kissed Mom before he headed to the Ministry of Education to meet his team.

They traveled in a small USAID van over a rugged road to Kandahar. Along the way, his Afghan colleagues listened in rapt attention to his every word, gleaned wisdom from his educational leadership. He asked them questions to get them to share, one of his secret ways to bond with people. At the age of sixteen, Morrie read Dale Carnegie's famous book *How to Win Friends and Influence People.* Dad added small comments to what the Afghans disclosed to encourage more conversation, then asked another question about them.

His goal to increase the literacy rate of the Afghan people made Dad anxious to see teachers beta test the pilot books with their students. In 1973, only 25 percent of the entire population read or wrote their own language, most of them children. This alarming statistic highlighted one reason why most Afghans' standard of living fell 200 years behind the rest of the world.

Dad believed childhood education was the most effective form of national security. He pointed out no matter how poor the children, they thrive if given opportunities since education develops innovative thinking plus the ability to analyze and express ideas. Dad proclaimed education the cornerstone to progress. To him, education enabled students to cross the fundamental differences between poverty and wealth in every country.

Once in Kandahar, my father conversed through his Afghan translators. Dad met dedicated teachers in a small cement school building. He enjoyed the classrooms, where the real learning took place.

The students, curious about the fair-skinned observer in their classroom, smiled, paid attention. Like all inquisitive children, they whispered about the visitors to their schoolroom.

Since their school day included Islamic religious prayer, the school required head coverings. Each young girl wore a simple white scarf on her head, the boys each wore colorful hand-woven skullcaps to signify their tribal orientation.

Dad studied the undeveloped directives the teachers demonstrated, saw numerous ways to improve the instructional system. He noted few visual or kinesthetic aids, like storyboards or maps, no counting tools for math. A single chalkboard hung on one wall.

Dad believed the more senses a child used while learning, the greater the comprehension and retention. He recognized teachers required a great deal of instruction. Therefore, he recommended they create a teacher's guide for each grade level.

Lunchtime arrived. Dad looked forward to the sack lunch Khan prepared. The school surprised him, invited his team into the tiny district office next to the school, where a huge banquet of food lay atop a bright red, hand-woven Afghan carpet. Main dishes, pilaf, egg, fruit, *naan* (bread).

The staff invited the men to kneel on the rug. Women teachers waited in another room. After the men finished, the women ate the leftovers.

The Afghan food smelled delicious, but Dad worried about food preparation. The lack of refrigeration and unsanitary water made him question whether to eat the unfamiliar food or not.

From his reading, he knew most Afghans suffered from dysentery all their lives, accepted it as normal. Because of this unhealthy digestive disorder, other fatal diseases, the average life of an Afghan citizen lasted only forty-four years.

They made Dad the honored guest. An attendant poured the first cup of green tea for him. Two heaping spoonfuls of raw sugar lay at the bottom of the cup of hot liquid. If unstirred, the pile of sugar melted into the brew, sweetened the tea enough to douse the bitterness.

A large brass platter held a mound of scrambled eggs, stacks of fresh-baked *naan* wrapped in colorful hand-woven cloth. A small platter held sweet *kharboza* melons, similar to honeydew, thin slices with the rind on. Dad thought about the sack lunch concealed in his briefcase. He imagined the reaction if he pulled out his sack lunch, ignored the feast. More essential than imagined illness, he took the opportunity to fit in with the other men. So, afraid he might insult his team, he chose to risk dysentery.

Dad scanned the feast on the red carpet, saw no serving utensils, forks, spoons, or chopsticks. They used only the right hand to eat and greet. They limited the left hand to wiping after defecating. If the police caught an Afghan thief, the state cut off their right hand, scarred them for life.

Haji demonstrated how to tear off a small tortilla-sized portion of *naan* with his right hand. The left hand gripped the fabric around the *naan*, never touched the warm flat bread. He used the *naan* like a mitt, scooped a handful of egg, ate it in two bites with his right hand like a taco.

Dad followed suit, dug his piece of *naan* into the pile of egg with his right hand. In most cultures, when people break bread together, a social bond forms between them. The educated men laughed together, enjoyed their plentiful lunch.

When he returned home exhausted from his first official business excursion, my father smiled, nodded his head, indicated a successful mission. With his knowledge of the fundamental inconsistencies in the educational system, he focused on solutions to narrow those gaps. The real work began.

After Dad told his tale of adventure, he pulled the stale sack lunch Khan prepared for him out of his briefcase. We all laughed. Dad patted his stomach, said, "So far so good."

Anxious to make critical changes to the student textbooks, develop learning guides for teachers, his team's receptiveness to his ideas encouraged Dad because Afghan educators worked in a suppressed environment, afraid to make decisions and take responsibility. The next morning, he outlined the relevant tasks. Number one, develop teachers' guides.

He arranged for language training from the Peace Corps. By his third month in the country, he spoke Dari like a four-year-old. "Cutler Luck" struck again. In a drawer at the Ministry of Education, he found an English translation of the first-grade stories. From those stories, he taught himself to read Dari script. He impressed the Afghan writers when he read, reviewed their second and third grade stories.

In Afghanistan, a Muslim country, my father didn't disclose to the men how written Dari resembled Hebrew and Yiddish. However, he did mention how learning Gregg shorthand in college assisted him to learn to read Dari. He found the language simple, because Dari used only two irregular verbs. The rest became a matter of learning vocabulary.

The Afghan writers wrote stories for the textbooks in Dari and Pashtu from themes my father developed. He wanted to make the books relevant to the culture. Because of Afghanistan's fabled history of early tribal conflicts, Dad included this rich history in the second and third grade books.

Over the centuries, the armies of Genghis Khan, Tamerlane, Babur terrorized the local tribes, devastated the farmers' water systems, prevented the development of any centralized system of government. In 1747, a local Afghan tribal leader, Ahmad Shah, led the household guards for the Shah of Persia. On the Shah's assassination, Ahmad Shah returned home with his men. Along the way, they took control of the city of Kandahar. His victory became a springboard to power as chieftain. He's known as the father of modern (I use this term loosely) Afghanistan.

Back at the Ministry of Education, Dad wanted to relate each story in the books to Afghan children. He soon recognized he couldn't study customs of family units in Afghanistan, because families did not go out together. They didn't walk to the mosque together. Women sat in isolated sections inside the mosque. Few women or girls appeared on the street. When they went to the bazaars, they covered themselves from head to foot with their *chadris*.

Chadris, a unique style of *burka* worn by many Afghan women, flowed from head to ankles. The lightweight cotton cloth draped a woman's body in an upside-down cone fashion. Women looked ghostlike in their flowing *chadris,* which came in a variety of colors, delft blue the most popular. A tight woven mesh covered the face and eyes—Muslims believed the woman's face, the most tempting part of her body, must always remain covered in public.

Afghan society gave women no respect. It treated them like objects, lower than dogs, required them to stay home to wash, clean, cook. In general, men shopped in the bazaars, controlled the money.

Society forbade little girls to do much, let alone appear in public without their mothers. They stayed home, cleaned, cooked, washed clothes. Those fortunate to attend school developed friendships while in school. Once school ended, they raced home for fear of reprimand or a beating if they failed to complete their chores.

Afghan boys experienced a much different childhood. They played like boys everywhere. It amused Dad how boys used their imaginations to play games made from trash or discarded items. He said it reminded him of his early years, when he and Uncle Alex played on the streets of St. Louis.

In one popular game, the boys rolled the rusted, mangled, metal rim of a bicycle wheel. Young boys used a stick to see how fast they could spin the rim down the rutted dirt roads. Entire gangs of boys ran alongside the rim tamer. If the group of boys found more than one bent rim, they raced against each other.

My father experienced great satisfaction when he wove Afghan culture into the stories in the books. He focused on the positive aspects of their way of life, not only to help the children relate to the story, but to help them build a sense of pride.

The Afghan writers approved Dad's initiative to include lengthy notes on how to conduct reading lessons in the teacher's guides. Printed motivational comments, thought-provoking questions added to class discussions with students. Positive feedback from teachers who used the experimental stories poured in through field representatives. The stories and teachers' guides proved an enormous success.

One Friday, Dad, two colleagues drove in the USAID van to a remote all-girls school in the hills on the outskirts of Kabul. USAID provided a van and driver whenever needed. More affluent Afghans lived in the city, while those less fortunate lived in the caverns in the mountains. This school beta tested the revised second grade books. Dad wanted to see the implementation of the books and teachers' guides in action.

At the end of the school day, Dad exchanged good-byes with a devoted second grade teacher. She asked him in Dari for a ride into Kabul. "My husband's in the army stationed in the capital and I can't ask an Afghan man." Each weekend, she commuted by bus into the city to see him at a cost of fifty cents round trip, the equivalent of one day's wage.

To ask an Afghan man to drive her meant disgrace.

Dad said, "Delighted to give you a ride in my van."

He sensed her upset, asked what troubled her. The teacher told my father one of her second-grade girls dropped out of school. Her family sold her to a fifty-year-old man to become his third wife. They planned to wed the next week.

Dad asked, "How can this happen?"

In Dari, the young teacher explained, "The older man paid several animals to buy her. Her family needed the money. Such a young wife made him a big man, because it meant he still got an erection."

The next week, while Mom volunteered at the maternity hospital for Afghan women, she observed the young age of many new mothers. Mom and several other Foreign Service women brought jars of powdered milk for expectant mothers. Mom discovered parents often sold young girls nine to twelve years of age to the highest bidder. Their families didn't want them, another useless mouth to feed. Adolescent girls got no say in their future, most never received the privilege of an education.

Because my father worked at the Ministry of Education, he met many semi-educated, earnest, dedicated individuals. The Afghan political and religious system held them back in their professions. Their form of Islam didn't allow the use of scientific methods because, "Allah provides." The man appointed to run the Ministry of Education made all the decisions, never asked for input from others. No one who worked for him dared make suggestions. Due to this autocratic procedure, they introduced few new ideas.

Dad's project through Columbia University allowed one Afghan educator at a time to attend, obtain an advanced degree in New York. When the educator returned to his homeland, Dad asked him how he applied his new knowledge. The simple outcome: he didn't. No higher up Afghan educator welcomed him back or asked how his new skills applied to improve their system. In such a closed society, little of the modern world ever appeared.

Once he discovered this problem, Dad designed the reading program for grades four, five, six to include stories with a technical twist. My father wrote about new ways to cure animal skins for clothes, new factories to dry fruit, new methods to farm crops.

When Dad approached Haji Tarin with his idea, Haji endorsed it. Dad overheard him discuss the idea with the other writers. Despite high enthusiasm, they did not know or understand the new technologies, making it difficult to write the stories.

Dad suggested they obtain specifics from knowledgeable professors at Kabul University. Dad pointed out every six weeks, members of the writing team also visited experimental classrooms around the nation. While on the field trips, he took his team to farms and factories to understand more of the processes. They liked this proposal a lot. This optimistic morale among the writers generated a positive jolt to the project. An upbeat buzz grew around the Ministry of Education.

The fourth-grade stories began with the writers in high spirits until they encountered a problem with the story of how people made silk. The Afghan writer who visited the silk makers, a cottage industry, on the outskirts of Kabul, found the process useful.

The writer composed an interesting story. However, Dad questioned the choice of terms when the writer described the three stages of the silk worm. Dad explained the cocoon hatches a moth, not a butterfly, according to the story in English.

The writer said, "Dari uses one word for both insects."

Dad said, "Let's check with the university advisor. If no separate word for moth exists, we'll create a new one."

The professor said, "Not permitted."

Through a letter, my father contacted the Asia Society Director in Iran, who found two separate words in Farsi. After a frustrating two-week wait for a response, the writers found this new word acceptable.

Every visit outside Kabul brought new ideas to the team. In Ashak, a small northern town outside of Mazar-i-Sharif, they discovered a new carpet weaving factory. Instead of women or young girls, men wove the rugs. In Kandahar, they learned of a factory with new machinery to weave rugs.

When they talked with the owner, they learned his previous supervisor opened a new factory for drying fruit. This owner spoke good English. He encouraged the farmers from whom he bought fruit to dry their fruit on reed mats. If they did this, he paid more because he didn't need to wash the fruit three times.

When asked how he marketed the fruit, he explained he transported the fruit by truck into the Soviet Union, then to Europe by train. The writers enjoyed learning about the new businesses in their country, responded with increased creativity.

While on the same journey, they found a pomegranate farmer and his adolescent son. Their roadside handmade hut displayed piles of crimson fruit for sale. A pomegranate tree shaded the hut. After he bought a sack of pomegranates, Haji gave the boy one of the fourth-grade books. "*Baksheesh*," he said. The boy asked in Dari, "Why do I need one?"

This ten-year-old boy never saw a book in his life, not even the Quran, which shocked Dad. The child expressed no opinion or values about written education, because he never experienced it. Haji said, "The *mullah* (head priest) at the mosque will teach the boy to read this first book to help him improve himself and his family farm."

Dad hoped this boy became an example for other children in their village. Enthusiasm for education needed to spread. The children needed to make it happen.

For the fifth grade, Dad established a set of five stories about Afghan heroes from the past. He created a list of names, asked his writing team to select their favorites. The *Pashtuns* wanted five of their heroes, the *Tajiks* wanted their five. Dad suggested two heroes from each tribe, then one famous person considered a neutral hero for all Afghans. When Dad offered the name Genghis Khan, he feared they'd throw him down the stairs. After hours of deliberation, Haji Tarin found a famous old medical man acceptable to everyone.

After six months, Dad designed a unique multiple-choice reading interest survey for teachers in every grade level. At three schools, they polled teachers, who had never been allowed to express their opinions, to determine what students wanted to read. Dad included the results in his six-month report to Columbia University. The professors in New York were elated to see this new data from the project's first reading interest survey.

Dad was asked to stay on two more years to complete textbooks for grades 7-12. He and Mom both agreed it was time to return to the US.

Uncle Alex accepted Dad's position and with the same team of Afghan educators completed the texts for higher learning through 12th grade.

Uncle Alex's previous role was developing curriculum to educate teachers at Kabul University.

By the time we left Afghanistan on June 30, 1975, the team had finished reading, writing, and math books for grades one through six. All children throughout the Islamic nation learned in a cohesive, formalized education program. They learned, developed thinking patterns, and gave back to their country in future years.

For my father, the opportunity to develop The Royal Curriculum for the Afghan people touched his life. His mantra: "Affect others in a constructive manner." His work at the Ministry of Education in Kabul opened a world of adventure and meaningful friendships.

17

HOME LIFE IN KABUL

At the start of our second month in Afghanistan, we settled into our permanent home on Darul Aman, one of the four paved roads in the country. Our spacious two-story home in Kārta Seh, surrounded by the customary eight-foot concrete retaining wall, the most beautiful we ever lived in, sat next door to the Afghan Parliament.

The front double doors opened into an elegant formal foyer tiled with earth-toned polished agate squares like marble. The first room to the right off the foyer housed built-in white cabinets. Matching floor to ceiling bookshelves covered the adjacent wall, perfect for Dad's home office.

Opposite Dad's office, the elegant tiled floor swept into the living and dining rooms. A wood-burning fireplace encased in a matching border of agate tiles highlighted the main wall off the sitting room.

Huge picture windows, a single glass door looked out onto our manicured yard. A large rectangular fountain in the center attracted natural wildlife. One afternoon while Dad and Mom enjoyed a cocktail in the garden, I counted 105 cherry trees planted around the greenery.

Soon after our move, Khan, our cook, asked Dad if his future brother-in-law, Ali Bosh, could work for us. Ali Bosh planned to marry Khan's wife's sister, but he lacked the money to pay her dowry. Khan explained the young couple fell in love, wanted to marry soon. When we met Ali Bosh, he spoke no English, but his warm smile, caring eyes won us over.

Our home in Kabul

Khan and Ali Bosh stayed in the separate two-room servants' quarters at the side of the house. Mom made sure they had all the amenities they needed. Khan went home every night to his wife and three small children, while Ali Bosh stayed over six nights a week. Khan relieved him one day each week, to allow him to see his family and fiancée.

From our upstairs bedroom windows, we saw Afghan dignitaries enter, leave the Parliament building. Dad gave me the master bedroom, a safe room at the back of the house. He

Summer in Kabul

and Mom moved into the larger of the two front bedrooms because Dad preferred a view of the front driveway with the Afghan Parliament building nearby. Together we shared a long cement balcony wrapped around the side, back of the house overlooking the lush garden.

The Soviet Embassy compound, where all the Soviets who work in the country lived, lurked a quarter mile up the street. Though we passed this ominous fortress daily, we Americans never stepped on the impregnable property.

USAID provided a generous selection of furnishings, sofas, chairs, beds, dressers, tables, lamps, rugs, all available from a warehouse in the USAID compound. Dad left the decorating decisions to Mom and me. We chose which fabrics to mix in each room. We customized the upholstered furniture to our taste, including pillows, drapes. Mom and I enjoyed playing interior decorator for our new home. The abundance of labor helped us complete all the work within a week.

Winter in Kabul

Dad chose to tutor Khan and Ali Bosh in English, which served several purposes, learn a second language, increase their employment opportunities, and communicate better with us at home. Every Tuesday and Thursday, Khan prepared dinner early. On those designated nights, Dad arrived home by 4:30 p.m. Khan and Ali spent ninety minutes at our dining room table learning from Dad. They practiced reading, writing, speaking in English.

After several months, Khan read the two-page *Kabul News*, delivered daily to all Foreign Service residents. They liked to read the stories about their cities. Both became dedicated students, studied their lessons, wrote out their assignments in the evenings. My father was proud of them.

Dad formulated an evening discussion group that included two of my teachers. Topics ranged from politics, religion, economy, humanity. Both teachers attribute this experience and Dad's influence to their pursuit of PhDs.

Every day brought a new adventure in Kabul. At dinnertime we shared daily escapades with one another. Mom escaped arrest several times during the two years we lived in Kabul. Due to her exotic looks, locals often mistook her for an Afghan woman. Although she wore modest clothing to conceal her arms and legs, she wore no veil. Mullahs, the head Muslim priests, spit at her in the bazaar to show their disgust.

One time, while she drove Khan into the bazaars to shop together, Afghan police stopped Mom because the law forbade women to drive a car with a man in the passenger seat. The police officer didn't see the diplomatic license plates, because he yelled at Khan, "Drive the car."

Khan shouted back in Dari, "I don't know how to drive the car!"

The police wanted to arrest Mom, take her to jail. Mom anticipated the officer's next move, pushed the automatic door lock before he tried to open her door. She hollered through the window, "Follow me to the American Embassy to arrest me."

The officer retreated. From then on, Dad teased Mom, "You're my Afghan wife."

Another time, my mother hired Khan's wife and sister to come to our home, sew *toshokhs* (thick blankets) for the brisk winter months. They showed up at our home five straight mornings, sewed by hand all day for a week. When on the third day Afghan police officers pounded on our door, demanded entrance, we guessed they put our house under surveillance. They thought Mom ran a house of ill repute, threatened to arrest her. She called the US Embassy, which sent two armed Marine guards to protect everyone.

Morrie in the back yard

My encounters, though meaningful, proved less exciting than Mom's. One day after school, I left a classmate's house to return home for dinner. After I stepped off the local bus, I walked along the rutted road toward our temporary home. Three short blocks from the house, I found a small dirt-covered cemetery. The 12-foot by 12-foot hardened clay plot of land sat between two houses. I neared the desolate markers in the soil, noticed an Afghan woman crouched under a tree. Her faded *chadri* billowed up like a mushroom in the cool breeze. Her cries for the loss of a loved one drew me to her.

I realized people, in general, behave the same around the world. We all love, we all grieve. I approached her step by step. She stood when she saw me. Exposed outside her *chadri*, her hands revealed a young woman. We exchanged words in Dari. She grieved the loss of her son. My heart sank from a quick memory of my brother Wayne.

Without hesitation, I reached into the back pocket of my Levis, pulled out my little money. My heart ached for her. I handed the woman twenty *afghanis* (two dollars). "*Baksheesh,*" I said. She took my hand in hers, sobbed words of thankfulness. I felt her gratitude. My heart filled, I knew I made a difference to this stranger.

At dinner, I shared the encounter with my parents. Dad told me the average Afghan earned the equivalent of forty dollars a year. Twenty *afghanis* bought her family rice for one month. Until then, other than donating toys, clothes to charity, I never gave money without conditions on my own. Dad always gave generous amounts of both his time and money, a wonderful role model.

By November, the first snow fell on the dusty city, colored everything white, my first frozen winter experience. However, winter in Kabul fell far short of a Norman Rockwell painting. The primitive Afghan lifestyle became more difficult during the harsh winter. Kabul sits at a higher elevation than Denver, Colorado's bitter cold climate. Because of a dockworker strike in Karachi, Pakistan, the shipment containing our winter clothes, essential household items waited in a sealed container on the docks on the Indian Ocean.

Friends told us about the "Nixon Bazaar," a used clothing bazaar with donations sent from the United States. We all laughed at the name, which changed over the years depending on the current President of the United States. We found the bazaar on the outskirts of Shari Nao. Each of us picked out a couple of jackets and sweaters, performed the ritual barter before we paid. After a few minutes, the shopkeeper told Dad in Dari, "Your wife and daughter barter like Afghans."

We all chuckled at the idea we performed our best bartering at the Nixon Bazaar.

Weeks earlier, Dad and Khan purchased two turkeys to raise for Thanksgiving and Hanukkah dinners. He watched the turkeys run around the yard, laughed at their dumb antics. Months before we left Los Angeles, the Watergate Scandal erupted. Dad, a strong Democrat, thought it fitting to name the turkeys Nixon and Agnew.

The day arrived to slaughter Nixon for Thanksgiving dinner. Dad and Khan acted like two little boys hatching a devious plot. When I spotted Dad holding a large cleaver, I decided to steer clear of the kitchen.

We invited several international friends to help us celebrate the American Thanksgiving feast. Mom and Khan prepared the traditional holiday cuisine. Dad carved the turkey, like every year. On Hanukkah a month later, Agnew tasted far better—he had more time to plump.

One chilly wintry day, I hung out with a school buddy of mine. The fire roared in his beautiful home in Wazir Akbar Khan. His father worked at the US Embassy. Whenever I stopped by, his mother showed me hospitality, friendship.

This day, I overheard his mother scream dreadful words to their cook. Shocking! My parents never spoke to our housemen in such harsh tones. Cultural and language differences, lack of experience, cause miscommunication between people. When they made mistakes, Dad and Mom always treated Khan and Ali Bosh with the utmost respect. They took time to demonstrate how they wanted tasks done in our home. The outcome: Khan and Ali Bosh reciprocated with loyalty, trust, kindness.

Ambassador Theodore Elliot and his charming wife Pat invited us to their residence for cocktail parties, pool parties. I loved the US Ambassador's extraordinary estate in Kabul. Expansive lawns surrounded the sprawling home. An Olympic-sized pool, covered patios for an enchanted party atmosphere, a basketball/tennis court in the back completed the estate.

No television, only one radio station, controlled by the Afghan government, existed in Afghanistan. For social entertainment, the foreign community participated in parties together. Every Monday evening, the Marine guards from the US Embassy hosted a happy hour. Mom and Dad gained popularity; people invited them to many dinner parties. They became regulars on the Kabul diplomatic social scene.

18

MAIL CALL

While we lived in Kabul, isolated from the modern world, we looked forward to mail delivery, our link to loved ones back home.

Mail delivery day turned into an event. My father's position with the State Department enabled us to receive our mail through the diplomatic pouch from Washington, D.C., which arrived on Ariana Airlines, the only airline into Kabul.

The government-owned airline operated three planes, one often not in service. When the company started operations in the 1950s, Afghans nicknamed the planes *Insha Allah* Airlines, hoped, "God willing," the plane took off, and landed safely.

The locked diplomatic mail pouch arrived at the US Embassy two times a week. Our mail went to Dad's office at the

Ministry of Education within twenty-four hours of arrival. In the stormy winter months, we went two weeks or longer with no mail because planes couldn't always take off or land in the icy mountain city.

On mail day, a treat for everyone, we received treasured gifts from family and friends. Their letters brought us a taste of the normal life we left behind. I loved to get our weekly letter from Bella, my paternal grandmother, then in her eighties.

Although Bella read and wrote English, she felt most comfortable in Yiddish. After dinner, the three of us gathered in the living room to read her narrative. Dad, the only one who read Yiddish script, read aloud. Mom and I translated the words into English to practice our Yiddish. Mom let me attempt a translation first, then she filled in the gaps.

Baba (Bella) conveyed each family member's *nakhas* (good fortune) or challenges. Although we lived on the opposite side of the earth, for a brief time each week, her letters helped us feel closer to family, conventional life.

Dad joked I received more mail than he and Mom put together. Not only did I correspond with many girlfriends and cousins, I also left behind a boyfriend who wrote me a new letter every day. He sent small gifts, occasional packages of my favorite candies like Tootsie Rolls, Red Vines, and Good and Plenty. Packages under one pound qualified for dispatch in the diplomatic pouch. I shared my bounty with Dad, who boasts a big sweet tooth.

One month, a letter from Terri arrived with her new living arrangements, wedding plans.

Dad longed to attend his eldest daughter's wedding, but he couldn't return to the states in July. For income tax purposes, he needed to stay out of the country for eighteen months or longer. If he met this criterion, he became exempt from income tax, which made his salary a good deal higher, one of several benefits to working overseas.

Terri chose not to change her wedding date. I flew back to Los Angeles the first week of June, stayed with my best friend's family in Northridge. Terri asked me to be her maid of honor.

Mom flew from Kabul to California three weeks later. She missed Nana Jennie, her aging mother, and Terri, who held her quaint wedding at a family friend's garden home in Northridge, a lovely celebration. We missed Dad.

19

FAMILY ADVENTURES

A few weeks after we moved into our new home in Kabul, Dad and Uncle Alex planned the trip of a lifetime for all of us. They rented a luxurious houseboat on the Kashmir River in northern India; the same houseboat Ambassador to the United Nations Adlai Stevenson stayed on in the early 1960's. It included a cook/houseman to look after our every need. My cousin Scott took leave from the Navy, flew in to join us on the adventure.

My first away cheerleading trip for my high school, AISK, took me to Islamabad, Pakistan two days prior to our vacation date. Dad arranged my travel plans. I flew from Islamabad to Lahore, Pakistan, where I planned to meet their flight, travel the remainder of the journey to India with the family.

Our football team won the tournament. The international school in Islamabad hosted a party for the visiting school. At the party, a friend introduced me to Benazir Bhutto and her younger brother Ali. In 1973, Benazir returned home on break from Harvard University. An elegant, stunning young woman with a confident friendly air about her, I knew she'd intrigue my father because their father held the post of Prime Minister of Pakistan. Later, in 1990, Benazir became the first woman to lead a Muslim nation.

The next morning, I caught my flight from Islamabad to Lahore, Pakistan. I wanted to see my family, vacation on the Kashmir River. From my itinerary, I had a two-hour wait in the Lahore airport before my parents' flight arrived.

My plane landed. I got off and everyone else in the airport boarded, leaving me alone in the waiting area. The airline official called me to his check-in desk. When I showed him my ticket and passport, he asked for the airport tax, equivalent to about ten dollars.

I showed him my cash, American dollars and *afghanis,* asked which he preferred. He asked the nature of my visit to Pakistan. After fifteen minutes of banter, I recognized we'd never reach an agreement. He ordered me to follow him.

He led the way to a small office by the check-in desk, took my passport and ticket, told me to wait, locked the door behind him.

My Mickey Mouse watch told me I waited in the sparse office for over an hour. At first, I remained calm, continued to sit on the uncomfortable chair, read my book.

I heard a plane land, rose to peer out the tiny window, my family's plane. They expected me to board. A moment of panic struck. What if the airline official refused to let me on the plane?

My parents didn't know I'd waited for them, but they can't leave without me.

I tried the doorknob again. Still locked. I needed my father. He'd know what to do. With my ear against the door, I heard faint voices in the adjacent room, but didn't understand the conversation.

I ran back to the window, stared at the airplane, hoped my family could see my face, willed the pilot to stay on the ground. I felt trapped. Full blown anxiety took over.

Thirty minutes later, a key clicked in the lock. The airline official opened the door. My Dad followed him in. I ran to him for a quick embrace. Dad told me to grab my things, get on the plane. "I'll explain later," he said.

The airline official, a greedy spirit, asked Dad for *baksheesh* for the release of his daughter. Dad ended up paying one hundred dollars for my ransom. Again, my hero father came through.

Buckled up for the flight to Amritsar, our first stop in India, Dad motioned for me to look out the window of the plane. We saw prisoners of war (POWs), not much older than me, march on the hot tarmac. Stained with dirt and sweat, their loose dingy clothes hung on thin dark bodies. The young men, chained together with metal shackles around their ankles, hands cuffed behind their backs, faced Pakistani soldiers armed with automatic weapons. I asked Dad, "Who are they?"

"My best guess, Bangladeshi POWs returned to their homeland after two years in prison camps."

In my sheltered life, I never came closer to war. This incident helped me appreciate the privileged life I led, thanks to my father.

All planes stopped in Amritsar, in the Punjab, before they flew on to Srinagar where we boarded our houseboat. Amritsar, the spiritual center of the Sikh religion, home of the magnificent Golden Temple, lies a few miles from the Pakistani border in northwest India.

The taxi pulled up in front of our hotel. I sensed a change. The large vivacious woman who greeted us in the lobby said she managed the big house. After Dad took care of the payment, she showed us to our room.

The large barren room housed eight cots on a cement floor. Six beds lay around the perimeter of the room, two in the center. A single light bulb dangled from the midpoint of the ceiling. The spirited woman made a comment about how the harmless alligator lizards on the walls ate mosquitoes. My heart began to palpitate. The mass of brown lizards, eight to ten inches long, big heads, beady eyes, looked like lizard wallpaper in the room.

I whispered to Dad, "I can't sleep in this room with lizards on the wall."

"You can for one night, no problem," he said.

All six of us followed the proprietor down the hall to the communal bathroom. Clean and decent, it served our purpose.

We locked our luggage in our communal room, hired three two-seater bicycle rickshaws to take us around the city and to see the Golden Temple. Scott and I shared our own, while our parents stayed together for the afternoon.

A charming mountain town, Amritsar offers the ultimate pilgrimage for Sikhs around the world. Construction of the Golden Temple's many levels began in 1570, took a century to complete. Over the years, Muslims performed part of the construction of the shrine then time after time destroyed the temple in battles. The temple represents a unique harmony between Muslim and Sikh architecture. Experts consider The Golden Temple one of the best architectural examples in the world.

At dinner, we shared our adventurous stories about the afternoon, the Golden Temple the unanimous highlight for each of us.

In the middle of the night, I woke everyone up, afraid to go to the bathroom because of the lizard wallpaper. Dad said he didn't mind. After we survived the night, the next morning we boarded our small plane to Srinagar.

On the dock of the Kashmir River, our houseman waited for us. His dark face glowed with a friendly smile of pearl white teeth. He welcomed us aboard, eager to serve.

We stepped into a sultan's den. Plush reds, bright oranges, royal purples exploded on the furniture, windows. Mosaic mirrors hung in every room. Tassels, beads, dangles adorned each piece of fabric. The boat included a full kitchen, dining room, three master suites, a living room with a fireplace, a sundeck. Pure Indian luxury.

For days, we floated like royalty along the river, absorbed nature's best. The great Himalayas, peaks snow-capped, rose on one side. The Pir Panjal Mountains dominated our view on the other, a spectacular panoramic landscape. In the evenings, we played games, laughed, told stories of our escapades. We relaxed, enjoyed every family moment together.

One day, we docked upriver to walk around the quaint town, ate lunch. A man invited us into a carpet factory, where skilled workers made hand-woven silk carpets. They hand-spun, hand-knotted every thread, created the softest, most elegant carpets we ever touched.

Back in Kabul, after our week of scenic relaxation with quality family time, Dad said, "Kashmir is the loveliest, most charming part of India."

To study children in their home environments, my father visited more than 30 primitive villages to meet and observe Afghan children of different tribes. He and Mom took me out of school because the experiences we encountered while we traveled far outweighed book learning, gave me opportunities to see the world through a new lens.

On the most memorable of these excursions, our trip to Bamiyan and Band-e Amir, we caravanned with two other families for safety. We ascended northwest from Kabul to Bamiyan, the historic site of ancient Buddhism. Hard to imagine this strict Muslim country the center of Buddhism for more than a thousand years.

Friends showed us photos of the great Buddhas carved into the sandstone cliffs of the Hindu Kush Mountains. The real Buddhas proved far more impressive than the prints.

On one of those picture-perfect days, we relished a picnic lunch at the base of the Buddhas. The sun shone high in the clear blue sky, warmed the air to a comfortable seventy degrees.

After lunch, three of us teenagers planned to climb through the dark, creepy caves, stand on the top of the large Buddha. We munched on homemade sandwiches while Dad told stories about the ancient Silk Road, the centuries-long crossroads of power, where Marco Polo, Genghis Khan, many other famed conquerors traveled on their way to greatness.

Afghanistan became a major branch of the Silk Road, where hundreds of thousands of traders carried luxury goods and ideas between Rome, India, China. Throughout the years,

Bamiyan grew into a pivotal axis for world religion, philosophy.

Morrie at Bamiyan, Afghanistan

My father said, "The Buddhist priests and their followers built these larger than life statues of worship around the sixth century AD, lived, meditated in the mountain caves."

Workers hewed the main bodies of the Buddhas into the sandstone mountain. The sculptures' details, constructed of a mud-straw mixture, lay on wooden armatures. Dad's explanation reminded me of papier-mâché projects I made in elementary school, only on a much grander scale.

Bamiyan Statue

Dad added, "After Islam appeared in the region in the seventh century, the religion spread for several hundred years. Mongol leader Genghis Khan led his massive army of 40,000 warriors to claim the city of Bamiyan in 1221. His army wiped out the faces of the Buddhas, obliterated the ancient Buddhist city of Bamiyan.

We finished our hearty lunch while the sun warmed our backs. The adults decided to play bridge on the natural rock formations in front of the Buddhas. Three of us took off for the caves.

I followed my friend Jimmy. We climbed higher into the caves, the light faded. None of us carried flashlights in the terrifying darkness. Nancy followed me. I felt more secure between my two friends. Bats flew across the caverns. Dozens hung upside down, watched us with their beady eyes. I thought about the old Alfred Hitchcock movies. We ascended, continued to talk, laugh. Our voices helped us all feel safer. Nancy held onto one of my ankles. I did the same with Jimmy. We wound around the curves, minute beams of light filtered into the caves, reassured us. We stayed close to the front of the Buddha, not too far into the cavern.

Fifteen minutes later, we reached the top of the large Buddha's head, took in a magnificent view of the Bamiyan Valley. The platform on the head looked the size of a round dining table for six. My eyes swept across the fertile green farmlands, the endless trail of the Hindu Kush Mountains, toward Pakistan. In the clear air, we saw for hundreds of miles.

For two hours, the three of us played cards, smoked hashish on the top of the Buddha's head. Etched into the cave above the Buddha's head we saw faint ancient paintings, thousands of years old. Of course, we told our parents we only played cards, talked about the old paintings in the caves, left out the hashish.

At night, we ate a traditional Afghan meal of kabob, *naan,* fresh fruit, checked into the *yurt,* a dome-shaped tent the size of a small bedroom, structured of thin wooden poles draped with cloth and animal skins. Dad said the *yurt* offered considerable warmth in the high mountain region. Eight of us stayed together in the *yurt*, each on a *charpoy* bed made of wood, wool twine. On top of each bed lay a *toshokh* (thick blanket) for padding, warmth, comfort. The night felt like a slumber party. With no electricity, we retired before the darkness settled. We snuggled into our *toshokhs*, shared stories, giggled until the wee hours of the night.

The next morning, we woke at dawn for the windy drive up the mountain to Band-e Amir, a series of six natural lakes unknown to most of the world. At 10,000 feet, natural travertine mineral walls divide each individual lake. Travelers call it the "Grand Canyon of Afghanistan."

At the base of Band-e Amir, we chose between horseback or walking up the narrow trail to view the lakes. Local Afghans told us the trail took three hours to climb. Neither Dad nor Mom chose to go. Dad didn't want his first experience on a horse to happen on this eight-inch wide treacherous trail.

Five of us decided to go up the steep trail on horseback. For fifty *afghanis* (five dollars per person), an Afghan boy or man on foot hand-led each horse. The Afghan man who took the money assured Dad in Dari the horses knew the trail, walked with care.

The horses walked upward along the dusty trail. We rocked back and forth in our saddles. Perspiration formed on my forehead, under my arms, part due to the warm sun, part to my tension. Most of the ascent, the path climbed at a steady forty-five-degree angle on a path no wider than the length of my foot, an inch beyond a sheer drop off the edge of the cliff. I told myself to relax, enjoy the view, yet I seldom looked down. Above, I saw either the butts of the horse and rider in front of me or the crystal-clear blue sky. I chose the latter.

My horse plodded along, maintained a perpetual climb. I gained confidence in the ten-year-old Afghan boy who led my horse. Ironic, at the same moment, my horse's front hoof slipped on loose rocks. My guide pulled on the rope, although the horse weighed a thousand pounds more than he did. He stumbled on the dirt, landed on his butt. My horse struggled to find solid ground with his outside front hoof. I held on tight. Loose rocks tumbled all the way to the base of the mountain. I leaned into the mountain, my courageous horse stabilized. We all took a deep breath. I thanked my guide in Dari, complimented his bravery to climb this mountain every day. I patted my horse's sweaty neck, told him the same.

After three hours, my horse rounded the top of the crest. I gasped at the spectacular beauty. Amid the brown and white cliffs, glimpses of sapphire blue flitted in and out of vision. I noticed sparse green bushes, thin at this higher altitude. My eyes focused on the distant view, a rich lapis blue danced on the glistening lake water. This perfect scene looked like a Hollywood backdrop. I never saw anything this beautiful made by nature.

The Afghan guides led our horses around the first three of the six natural lakes. Each lake had deeper, bluer tones than the previous one. We dismounted our horses, gathered around our guide in the shade of a large boulder. In Dari, he said, "The concentration of minerals forms the lake's rich, royal blue hues."

Dad loved places like Band-e Amir Lakes. I knew he and Mom hung out in the village below, engaged with children at play. While our guide spoke, I imagined Dad chatted with the children and their parents. All Afghans found life difficult, yet the citizens in cities faced different challenges than those in small villages. I hoped Dad could further his insight into what it meant to grow up Afghan.

Although the warm temperature warranted a jump into the lake to cool down, the frigid waters deterred me. Instead, I sipped handfuls of pure water to quench my thirst, with wet hands patted my face, arms, neck. The natural breeze cooled my body.

I gazed up at the horizon, inhaled the fresh mountain air. Stunning beauty surrounded me. The Afghans allowed the horses to meander in the shaded areas after they drank in the lake. The guide shared stories of Band-e Amir and Bamiyan with us, reminded me of my father, the great storyteller. My mind wafted to other spectacular vacation sites I visited with Dad. Of everywhere we traveled in the world, the lakes of Band-e Amir won first prize for natural beauty.

We took many other trips around Afghanistan monthly. Several times we traveled by car through the rugged Khyber Pass between Afghanistan and Pakistan, the lower section of the two-lane highway through the Kabul Gorge. On the road in our crème colored Toyota Corolla, Dad chuckled when we came upon a road sign suspended on a single metal pole no bigger than a flattened shoebox, hung at the top of a dusty crest. On it I saw two pictures, a line divided them, one side a silhouette of a camel guided animal traffic to the dirt road, the other, the rudimentary shape of a car directed autos toward the pavement. Only in Afghanistan. Life changed on the Marco Polo trail. Dad joked about this funniest road sign he ever saw for years.

20

INTERNATIONAL NOTORIETY

In the summer of 1974, after a month apart while Mom visited with family and attended Terri's wedding, she flew into Vienna, Austria to reunite with Dad.

They shared a luxurious suite at the Renaissance Hotel in this romantic city famous for its classical music, dancing, delicious coffee, a blend of imperial and modern architecture, like a Harlequin Romance.

Dad flew to Vienna from Kabul to speak at the World Reading Conference. This world-class global conference honored my father, one of the distinguished international speakers. They provided translation headsets for every attendee in fifty-seven languages. His colleagues from a multitude of countries spoke on innovative concepts in reading. The conference shared ideologies, theories, practices to improve reading instruction in schools, increase the literacy rate around the world.

Conference Board members invited Dad to be a guest speaker based on his reputation and the learning programs he developed while Principal at Van Ness and Encino Elementary Schools. He spoke on "Volunteers in the Schools." A tremendous controversy raged around whether to invite non-professionals like parents into the schools to work with students, because many educators felt parents were unqualified to teach. Dr. Lantz, Superintendent of Schools for Los Angeles Unified School District, submitted an article about my father's use of volunteers, shared conclusive results: significant improvement in primary students tutored by volunteers.

At the World Reading Conference, my father shared his experiences. He spoke with confidence, authority, frankness, compassion.

He started his first assignment, Principal at Van Ness Elementary School in the old Hollywood area. It's a coincidence Mom attended the same school in 1941, along with the kids from the movie *Our Gang*. In his short three years at Van Ness, Dad recruited three mothers who assisted many students who struggled with basic reading, writing, and math. He took a special interest in kindergarten through third graders who fell behind in their classwork, designed a tutorial program for each grade. The district used the school auditorium only for occasional assemblies, student performances. Dad placed three tables in the corners, one for each volunteer mom. Selected students received thirty minutes of tutoring each day from these dedicated volunteers.

Without comment, Dad showed his international audience his students' phenomenal test scores on the overhead projector. A buzz of voices filled the auditorium. Individualized one-on-one help each day proved beneficial to every student.

After my brother Wayne passed, Dad transferred to Encino Elementary School, a more affluent community, with higher educated parents. In the first year, Dad recruited over 100 volunteer mothers from active P.T.A. members. My father and one of the mothers, a USC graduate in Special Education, created a diagnostic test for each new kindergartener.

They designed the test to show whether a child needed help in four areas: visual, perceptual, kinesthetic and/or patterning. Kindergarteners who scored below seventy-five percent on the assessment received thirty minutes of individual practice each school day.

First, second, third graders used similar assessment tests. Over 100 moms rotated through the week, hundreds of students benefitted from their support. In his cool, nonchalant manner, Dad posted students' year-end test scores on the projector. Again, the audience buzzed.

For fourth, fifth, sixth grades, several moms became ecological promoters. Volunteers taught the importance of preserving our eco-system. In 1971, Encino became the first school in the Los Angeles basin to teach how to care for planet Earth, make it thrive. Students learned to explore, discover, think in terms of nature.

Because students showed overwhelming excitement to uncover more ecological information, the moms took their campaign to a new level. In conjunction with See's Candies, the volunteers launched a huge fundraiser to raise money to purchase young trees indigenous to other countries. The students then planted the trees at Libbit Park, a few blocks from the school. Students researched, selected trees based on climate zones and which trees attracted wildlife. The community welcomed beautiful shade trees to adorn the park, offset carbon emissions on our planet.

Dad told his audience students developed school pride, an eagerness to help their community, made a small contribution to slow global climate change. They also learned how to take care of the environment, a vital responsibility for every community member.

Always the storyteller, Dad shared a story about one exasperated father who approached him after school with his checkbook in hand. He said his son and wife drove him crazy over a See's Candies sale. He wanted to write a check for whatever the school needed. The audience chuckled. Dad said he thanked the gentleman for his willingness to help. Then he explained the fundraiser taught his son and other sixth graders to take an active role in their community, not take a handout from Mom or Dad. My father believes this made a lasting impression on many Encino students.

Assisted by scores of volunteers, Encino students also wrote a Proclamation to then-Governor Ronald Reagan in Sacramento. They impressed officials in Sacramento. The governor invited the sixth graders of Encino Elementary School to present their Proclamation in person.

Dad insisted all sixth graders go but earn their own way, which resulted in more fundraising. Teachers and parents helped students work toward their goal. When the students made the trip to the California State Capitol, they also visited

Sutter's Mill, where locals first discovered gold in California in 1848. After students returned from their big adventure, they built enough enthusiasm in the student body to make the fundraiser a sixth-grade tradition from then on.

Through the generous help of school volunteers, students became excited about preserving the environment, learned valuable research skills. Students increased their awareness of environmental issues, developed critical reading and writing skills through their written reports. For decades, the non-native arboretum of trees in Libbit Park grew larger every year, offered shade to the Encino community.

Some of the volunteer moms, inspired by my father's hard-working nature, decided to spruce up the school auditorium without permission. They bought paint, spent several hours painting the front of the auditorium around the stage. The custodian clued Dad in on the covert operation in the west wing of the school. He wandered into the auditorium.

He liked the stage's fresh new look. With his sarcastic humor, he startled them, said, "You left your maids at home to clean the house, so you could paint the school auditorium?"

The volunteer moms laughed, asked how he liked their work. He thanked them, complimented them on a job well done.

This international community of educators received my father's points with enthusiasm. The year-end test scores justified the volunteer tutoring program. More important, students gained self-confidence, their self-esteem reached new heights. At the World Reading Conference, Dad displayed a new way to bridge the gap between schools and parents. This result follows the adage: It takes a village to raise a child.

After the conference, Dad planned an exciting European journey for Mom. First, he rented a car. They drove around Austria, played tourist. They drank ample cups of mellow roasted coffee, visited the city of Salzburg, home of the musical prodigy Wolfgang Amadeus Mozart and the Von Trapp Family. My parents ran on the beautiful green hilltop where Julie Andrews sang, *"The hills are alive with the sound of music."*

Next, they spent two days touring the historic landscape of Yugoslavia. Dad marveled at old architecture mixed with modern designs among spectacular scenery. He navigated down the windy cliffs toward the Adriatic Sea. The warm summer weather attracted many Germans on holiday along this beautiful coastline. Everywhere they went—restaurants, shops, hotels—they encountered the same groups of friendly German vacationers. Dad took pleasure talking in his broken German with these people.

From there, he wanted to take Mom to Greece, but the war in Cyprus made it unsafe to travel in the region.

Back in Vienna, they turned in their rental car, flew to Israel for one week. Arye Ben-Gurion, nephew to David Ben-Gurion, the first Prime Minister of Israel, greeted them in Tel Aviv. Three years earlier, Dad forged a bond with Arye at his cousin's home in Los Angeles. Arye invited Dad to visit Israel.

Arye planned a historical tour for my parents. The first two days they lodged with Arye's cousins in Tel Aviv. When they visited Old Jerusalem, Dad soaked in the rich history. He pointed out to Mom the French Convent, the First Station of the Cross, where Pilate condemned Jesus to death. In the evening, Arye took them to the rooftop of a historic building to watch Jerusalem go to sleep. For a sacred moment, underneath the stars, Dad inhaled, smelled the bountiful history of the holy land.

The next day they visited Bethlehem, swam in the Dead Sea. For the first time in his life, Dad floated in water because of the high salt content. Under the Falls of Solomon, they rinsed the salt off their bodies, drove to the kibbutz founded by Arye and his wife.

The last two and a half days in Israel, Arye and his wife hosted my parents in their two-bedroom apartment on the kibbutz. The orderly life on the kibbutz fascinated Dad. Since the 1950's, when Arye and his family procured this raw plot of desert, they turned it into a gorgeous mini-metropolis. They grew fields of wheat, cotton, many fruits and vegetables, owned their own dairy. The kibbutz supported itself with manufacturing plants, schools, housing.

Breakfast and dinner featured kosher dairy products. The big banquet eaten in the middle of the day included chicken in abundance. The plentiful food at each meal allowed everyone to eat until satisfied.

Arye kept a historical library about Israel in a room attached to his apartment. He archived births, marriages, deaths of everyone who lived on the kibbutz. Arye also toured the small country to conduct classes on how to operate a proper kibbutz. Dad liked to philosophize about history with this knowledgeable, humble man.

The first night, Dad undressed, placed his shoes under the bed, felt a long metal object. His sense of touch identified a rifle. To avoid alarming Mom, he chose not to mention it to her. In the morning, he asked Arye about the firearm. Arye said in the pioneer days on the kibbutz, the members experienced frequent terrorist attacks at night. Since then, everyone over the age of sixteen on the kibbutz kept a rifle under his or her bed.

His experience in the holy land enriched Dad's life. He admired Arye for all he brought to Israel's people. Departure day arrived. He flew back to Kabul with renewed determination to help Afghanistan.

21

MORE ADVENTURES

In March of 1975, Dad flew home for two weeks to attend my grandmother Bella's memorial service. A dark cloud of sadness passed over him, he'd never see or speak with his ninety-year-old mother again. Because of her remarkable sense of logic and wisdom, he considered her a role model. No matter what their background, Bella saw the good in other folks.

We attended the intimate memorial service in the Los Angeles Synagogue. Every living friend and relative attended. Both Uncle Alex and Dad spoke of how their mother affected their lives. We celebrated her absolute love for others and her eventful life.

While home on leave, Dad attended several parties in his honor. With his boyish charm, my father fascinated his long-time friends with tales of his overseas experiences. Most of his stories sounded like fiction, but I knew their truth.

On his flight back to Kabul, Morrie recalled his visit to Los Angeles, a wonderful time to re-engage with family, good friends. On the other hand, he realized how acclimated he became to a simpler life in Kabul. The contrast between the primitive culture in Afghanistan and the "excessive luxury" of a big city most Americans took for granted staggered him.

Six weeks later, I flew back to Kabul to join my parents for one last month of living this extraordinary adventure. I wanted Terri to join me, but she and her new husband planned to buy a home, didn't want to dip into their savings.

My father and his team of writers completed the six levels of reading textbooks on schedule. Local educators used his teaching guides, learned innovative strategies for teaching thought-provoking lessons. A new generation of students learned to not memorize information, but to think, apply and formulate new ideas. Dad wanted these books to help Afghanistan's people learn about the modern world.

The Afghan Ministry of Education embraced the formalized reading program my father helped put in place. It offered educational uniformity throughout the country for all youngsters. The progress delighted Columbia University and the State Department. The United States, led by President Gerald Ford, on good terms with Afghanistan, aligned itself with the land-locked nation.

We felt the strengthened presence of the Soviet Union in Afghanistan. Afghan President Daoud became a mere puppet of the Soviet government. Soviet leader Leonid Brezhnev sought control of a southern port on the Indian Ocean, targeted

Afghanistan and Pakistan to achieve his goal. Dad heard from credible sources about Soviet plans to invade Afghanistan, push their way into Pakistan.

After two years in Afghanistan, my father didn't want to leave. The three of us grew closer than ever, created many special memories in this unique environment. Dad cultivated bonds with American diplomats and other Foreign Service personnel in Afghanistan. He grew to love a country not his own because of the mutual respect and admiration he developed with his Afghan colleagues. Yet he also felt a need to return to California with his wife and children to take on a new challenge.

When he prepared to leave, he knew his purposeful work made a significant difference to many students. Afghan educators acknowledged he'd completed his work in this antiquated country. The torch passed to his colleagues at the Ministry of Education.

Mom donated most of our household items to the American thrift shop, one-way international workers exchanged American merchandise with one another. Most of the proceeds from the thrift store went to help Afghan women at maternity hospitals.

The State Department offered to pay for the entire return flight up to 20,000 miles. Dad decided he wanted to experience one last tour before we landed in California. In our last few weeks in Kabul, we planned an exciting month-long trip through five Asian countries.

We said our good-byes to Khan and Ali, our trusted housemen. Dad secured positions for them with another family, gave them a generous tip for the hard work and dedication they showed us. We exchanged addresses with our close friends in Kabul, promised to write. In the diplomatic community's transient world, everyone knew people arrived and left often. My father, a seasoned traveler, taught me to make friends fast, because friendships often only last a brief period. On July 12, 1975, we departed from Kabul, headed for our home in Northridge, California.

Our five-country journey started in Katmandu, Nepal. We flew over the snow-covered Himalayas, listened to Dad talk about the ancestors of the Nepalese people, who dated back over 2,000 years. Near the flight's end, the pilot announced our approach to Mount Everest on our left. Passengers on the right side of the plane unbuckled their seatbelts, stood in the aisle. Everyone looked out the windows. We circled the majestic peak, which stands 29,029 feet tall, three times. What an awesome sight! I told Dad two months earlier I saw a documentary about Sir Edmund Hillary, the first Westerner to climb Mount Everest. Here we flew thirty thousand feet in the air, the only way for us to see the top of this storied peak.

Dad arranged for us to lodge at the USAID compound. Nothing luxurious, but comfortable. We enjoyed a hearty dinner, although Dad said anything topped Afghan food, I agreed. USAID staff told us to not wander the streets of Katmandu after dark.

The next day, the early morning sun glistened on temples around the city. Flickers of golden rooftops transcended the panoramic landscape. Katmandu provided an enchanted blend of two cultures, two religions, Hinduism and Buddhism. Old British traditions permeated the customs, yet the caste system remained in place.

Dad found the Nepalese people friendly toward us, happy by nature. Since Mount Everest attracted a constant parade of international climbers, the locals always welcomed foreigners. Nonetheless, stinky animal dung littered the city streets, which Dad found offensive. Sheep, goats, yaks, other animals roamed alongside their owners, like American frontier days when fur trappers filtered through town to trade their wares for supplies.

My father noted the difference between Katmandu and Kabul. In the Afghan city, people scraped up all animal dung to use to cook and heat. Dad noted the contrast between the terms "underprivileged" and "impoverished," Nepalese people the former, and Afghans the latter.

Our second morning, before we shopped in the bazaars, Dad told Mom and me, "A typhoon's approaching the area. Everyone return to the USAID compound by late afternoon."

I found shopping in Katmandu humorous, adventurous. Tiny Kama Sutra erotica shops, four to five a block, showed up all over the city. Mom didn't buy any erotic items, but she did find an intricate carved bone dragon the size of a wine bottle minus the spout on a custom sculpted stand. She displays this work of art in her living room today, one of my favorites from her collection.

Dad caught up with us a short while later. I needed time to spread my wings independent of my parents for the afternoon. We agreed to meet back at the hotel by five to avoid the typhoon.

Later, while we sipped a nice chardonnay before dinner, we listened to the violent rainfall pour down. The typhoon arrived on the scene like the Wicked Witch of the West in *The Wizard of Oz*. The fireplace roared, hypnotic flames danced over the wooden logs, offered a cozy environment to our family.

Dad encountered numerous typhoons in the South Pacific. He expected the storm to pass through the mountains by morning. When he inquired about my afternoon, my face lit up. Between bites of roasted chicken, herbed rice, sautéed leeks, I shared an incredible experience.

On a stroll near the main quad of a small marketplace, eight little boys, dressed in their faded blue and white school uniforms, approached me. None of them wore shoes, most looked in need of a bath. I happened to wear a royal blue T-shirt given to me by an Olympic athlete who stayed with us for ten days in Kabul. (Dad volunteered to house one of the nine visiting track and field athletes from the American Olympic team, who came to Kabul to assist Afghan athletes set up their own Olympic team.) My T-shirt said U.S.A.

The ten-year-old boys practiced their English with words like, "Ello Misez," and "I luff u." Mom and Dad chuckled at my imitation.

I told them how I reached into my woven purse, gave the boys sticks of Wrigley's gum, which bonded our friendship. The tallest of the boys spoke a few broken sentences of English.

Within minutes, the cluster of boys who gathered around me began to part. I looked over their brown shaved heads, saw an impeccably groomed boy, about the same age, walk toward us. His crisp ironed white shirt, royal blue short pants led me to believe he came from wealth. I noticed his polished brown shoes, knee-high socks. The tallest boy whispered to me, "Brahmin. He is smart."

Three months earlier, I read *Siddhartha,* a novel by Herman Hesse. This work of fiction deals with the caste system and the spiritual journey of an Indian man at the time of the Buddha. The philosophical book came to life for me. I realized these young boys believed a person born into a higher caste must be smarter.

The Brahmin boy spoke perfect British English. After a brief introduction, he offered to take me on a tour of the underground temples in the city. He spoke with no sign of arrogance, only self-confidence. After I asked the distance to the temples and whether we needed to travel by bus or taxi, he said, "We will walk."

I told Mom and Dad, "I felt like the Pied Piper. These cheerful little boys walked behind me down the tiny cobblestone alleys."

Dad asked if I played my flute. I smiled.

Within ten minutes, the boys approached the entrance to a Buddhist shrine with me. Multiple pairs of shoes lay on the first stone step down to the place of worship. I slipped off my sandals, set them alongside the others. The young Brahmin gestured for me to wash my feet under the waterspout before I entered the holy grounds.

The magnificent shrine held gold everywhere. The smell of incense filled the six-by-eight-foot room. I noticed the low ceiling, perhaps because most Buddhists tended to shortness in this region. Bowls of fruit lay in front of the hefty golden Buddha. We remained silent inside the temple. I watched each of the boys kneel, perform an unspoken ritual of prayer, then I followed them out.

Together, we visited five different Buddhist temples. My Brahmin friend said, "Welcome to Nepal, birthplace of Siddhartha Gautama, later Buddha or "The Enlightened One."

I lived a dream from the book I read.

Dad regretted he missed this opportunity. We only stayed three nights in this captivating mountain city, plenty of time to absorb the blissful harmony between two diverse cultures. Despite animal dung in the streets, the people's hearts exuded warmth, friendliness.

On our flight out of Katmandu, the pilot circled around Mount Everest three times, the opposite direction this time, gave us another glimpse of the most majestic mountain in the world.

Our next stop: Delhi, India to visit the famous Taj Mahal.

We woke to summer heat. After we showered in the luxurious hotel with the air conditioning on full blast, sweat soaked through Dad's white short-sleeved linen shirt.

He arranged for a car and driver to take us to Agra, two hours south of Delhi, to see the Taj Mahal, one of the New Seven Wonders of the World. On the drive, Dad filled us in on the history of the Taj.

In the early 1600s, Emperor Shah Jahan, grandson of the great Mughal ruler Babur, brought great wealth, prosperity to his people. He fell in love, married his princess before his father, the king, died. When his father took ill, Shah Jahan competed with his brothers for the throne. After several years of battle, both of his brothers died of suspicious causes.

Emperor Shah Jahan ruled in peace with his queen Mumtaz Mahal, Muslim leaders in a land where many practicing Hindus lived. The largest, most precious gems mined from India's soil encouraged a reputation of outrageous opulence. Together, they raised fourteen children, headed the wealthiest dynasty in the world. After the birth of their youngest, the queen took ill, died. On her deathbed, the Emperor vowed to build her a mausoleum more beautiful than any ever seen.

When we stepped out of the car, we saw masses of people swarm around the gates of the mausoleum. Emaciated cows roamed about, while the maimed and the poor begged for money.

We walked toward the entrance. I gasped, grabbed Dad's arm. To the right of us stood two nomadic women in Kuchi attire, one held the reins of two goats and a camel at rest. Both women wore enormous raw gold nuggets, the size of bananas, pierced into their ears, caused the skin of their lobes to stretch down to their shoulders. Dad explained this loaded tribe wore their wealth.

The gardens and reflection pool looked picture perfect, but the muggy weather made Dad joke he wanted to jump into the sacred pool to cool down. The closer we walked to the glistening white marble structure, the more magnificent it appeared.

Inside the Taj Mahal, a stunning piece of architecture, we saw tiny marbled tiles, each no bigger than a credit card, pressed with inlaid precious, semiprecious gemstones with pictures of various flowers, birds, Mughal designs. The motifs reached far beyond traditional elements. Emeralds, rubies, sapphires, many other jewels lined the walls of this enormous lapidary mausoleum.

Across the Yamuna River lay the Red Fort, built one hundred years before the Taj. My father said, "Soon after Shah Jahan completed the mausoleum, one of his sons overthrew his regime. The Emperor, grief-stricken at the death of his beloved wife, abdicated the throne. His son, the new Emperor, imprisoned his father in a tiny room of the Red Fort facing the Taj Mahal. The only window, a small broken piece of glass, allowed him to peer across the river while he dreamed of his lost love.

After three days in Delhi, we flew to Yangon, Myanmar (Burma). Dad reserved a hotel room on Yangon Lake. The area, a water reservoir created by the British in 1883, evolved into a famous location for romance and culture.

We grabbed a quick breakfast at our hotel, met a delightful Australian couple. Since Dad and Mom made friends wherever they touched down in the world, Dad invited them to tour the old-world city with us. They accepted.

The buildings on the riverfront resembled those of 19th century Great Britain. Our destination: the famous golden Shwedagon Pagoda. Melodious Burmese music blared from one of the old buildings, drew us like magnets.

Through the open door, we saw a young minority tribe practice their native dances. When the group noticed us, they invited us to dance with them. The adults bowed out, but Dad encouraged me to join in.

Two of the young tribal women gave me a warm welcome, pulled my arms to join them. The dancers spoke no English. I spoke no Burmese. I felt an instant bond, like three teenage girls at a high school dance. Together we made dance our universal language. They demonstrated; I followed their moves. Mom, Dad, and the Australian couple sat in chairs. The unique hand and leg movements differed from other dances I learned for my cheerleader performances. My muscles tightened, stretched while my body moved into Zen-like positions. After a few minutes, the leader of the dance group placed small flat glass candleholders in each of my moist palms. White votive candles sat on the top of the glass plates. Without air conditioning, after thirty minutes of practice I worked up a good sweat. The leader directed the dancers to light the candles for a dress rehearsal. One of the girls lit mine too. To maintain lit candles in my open palms while I twirled my hands, legs, full body proved a challenge in both artistic and athletic senses.

The dancers exuded genuine gratitude when we showed interest in them. In turn, we appreciated their warm kindness, said our goodbyes.

Dad said, "This Traditional Candlelight Dance is performed at all Buddhist festivals, holidays."

We meandered along the busy waterway, watched the locals in action, felt the serenity of this Asian scene. Yangon overflowed with harbor charm. Fishermen delivered their catch of the day, sailed their *junks* (small boats) up to the riverfront restaurants. Dad said he looked forward to fresh fish, a specialty in Yangon, famous for shellfish—not the kosher meal a Jewish boy from St. Louis might eat!

A few blocks from the water, we saw the Golden Pagoda across the city. I noticed Dad's stride increase the closer we got to the brilliant landmark. The tall golden *stupa,* an easy to locate beacon, guided tourists to this holy place from anywhere in Yangon. Much of the pagoda's beauty derived from the geometric marble complex, topiary landscape, yet the intricacy of the golden *stupa,* stretched high in the air, grabbed my attention.

A Buddhist monk, barefoot, shaved head, traditional bright orange cotton robe slung over one shoulder, greeted us in British English at one of the four entrances. I whispered to Dad, "Wonder if they wear underwear beneath the robes." He smiled, shook his head. Seated cross-legged, scattered through the marbled quad, Buddhists prayed.

When Dad looked up in amazement at the dazzling gold *stupa* on top of the pagoda, he realized it reached five stories high. The lower portion featured 8,688 solid gold bars, the larger upper portion another 13,153 bars of gold. The tip of the *stupa*, far too high for the human eye to see without binoculars, included 5,448 diamonds, 2,317 rubies, sapphires, other gemstones, 1,065 golden bells, at the top, a single 76-carat diamond, astonishing opulence.

After we absorbed the spiritual benefits of Buddhism at the Shwedagon Pagoda, we headed to the Burmese National Museum. The concierge at our hotel told Dad, "Worth your time."

When we entered through a small side door, the worn-out building looked unimpressive. The first floor housed artifacts thousands of years old. A few steps later, we saw the magnificent Royal Lion Throne, gilded in gold, 1800 years old, named after the carved golden lions perched on either side of the imperial chair where generations of Burmese kings sat.

We climbed up a tiny dark flight of stairs with no handrail to a room filled with a menagerie of fossils, carved jade, coral, ivory, ancient jewels from former dynasties. Even with a ninety-degree temperature and high humidity, we appreciated the historic significance of what we witnessed.

A few days later, we celebrated our arrival in Bangkok, Thailand. Dad joked about food when we ate hamburgers and French fries for the first time in years. The city offered fine dining, custom-made Western clothing, Western music, dancing, pasteurized milk, reminded us of the comforts of home.

We lodged at the USAID compound in the heart of Bangkok. The first day, Dad ordered two custom-fitted suits with the finest fabrics, picked them up two days later. Mom and I also took advantage of inexpensive tailor-made clothing. On our last day in Thailand, Dad sat on our suitcases to close them.

We pigged out on Thai food. My father loved Tom Yum Kung, the most famous of all Thai soups. It featured all four of the Thai spices—salty, sour, sweet, spicy—in every slurp.

One day, Dad arranged a car and driver to take us to Khao Yai National Park, about 100 miles northeast of Bangkok. The park featured the lush rainforest, an untamed tropical jungle. The freshest scents emanated from the thick forests, open grasslands of this balanced eco-system.

Dad told us the park hosted over 153 different species of animals, including wild elephants, tigers, leopards. We walked through the dense covered trails, heard waterfalls, exotic birds, animals. Larger than life insects crept along the trails. Dad turned over a giant elephant ear leaf to show me an ugly grasshopper which munched on the rich green foliage. Flowers of every color filled our nostrils with sweet fragrance. We tasted new varieties of fruit. I rode an elephant.

After four days amid the wonders of Bangkok, we flew to our last destination on the Asian tour, Singapore's Shangri-La Hotel, grand, luxurious, elegant, near tropical gardens next to the shopping district. We walked everywhere, including the theater, where Dad chose the movie *Towering Inferno*. We watched the dramatic movie in English with Mandarin subtitles.

The government of Singapore, an island twelve miles in diameter off the tip of Malaysia, keeps every street immaculate through enforcement of strict laws forbidding gum chewing on the streets or spilling garbage.

While dining our first night, Dad and Mom met a charming couple native to Singapore. The gentleman owned an import business, the woman taught school. They formed an instant friendship, offered to play tour guide. My parents accepted their offer with delight. For the next two days, the four of them toured the most historic sites on the island.

One of my friends worked at the American Embassy. Jack and I continued our friendship through letters after the government transferred him from Kabul to Singapore. While Dad and Mom enjoyed the island their way, Jack showed me the Singapore nightlife.

The exceptional beauty and traditional splendor of the island of Singapore made the perfect transition before we headed home to California.

22

FINDING HIS RHYTHM

Dad found it more difficult to readjust to conventional life than he anticipated. In three days, he needed to hire painters for the house, buy a car, contact all the utility companies. The renters paid on time but left the house in shambles.

From Honolulu, Mom made a detour, flew straight to Oakland. After more than a year away, she wanted to see her aging mother Jenny and sister Tamara.

Dad said, "I'll take care of the house before I report to my new school."

I joined Mom for two days of shopping for new clothes, returned to help Dad supervise workers at the house.

Los Angeles Unified School District appointed Dad Principal of Normandie Elementary School in South-Central

Los Angeles, a commute of forty-one miles each way from Northridge. He purchased an economical car, became acclimated to his new surroundings before he took on a new school, staff, students, and new parental concerns.

He worked under the same school district policies and procedures as at Encino Elementary two years prior. To apply these policies at a school of over 1,500 elementary students with forty-five teachers in the inner city was a daunting task for any principal.

1975 marked the year civil rights regulations required integration of blacks and whites in Los Angeles. This upset black parents because their children ended up riding the bus for thirty minutes or longer to and from school. This outraged whites because they moved to certain neighborhoods based on the outstanding academic reputations of the schools. They also paid higher property taxes for their homes. Many believed busing in children who possessed different mentalities, attitudes, and behaviors tarnished their perfect children, perfect schools.

When he prepared his talk for the first teachers' meeting at Normandie, Dad felt overwhelmed, a symptom of culture shock. It seemed ironic to feel more distressed when he returned to his homeland than when he moved to an undeveloped foreign country where he didn't know the language. The management responsibilities at school didn't change. Two years in Kabul changed my father. His thoughts became more global. Even though Normandie Elementary included one of the poorest neighborhoods in Los Angeles County, students had much more than Afghan students. In his first few weeks, Dad felt out of touch with the issues students at Normandie faced.

I supervised the workmen at the house until Mom arrived the day before the movers brought all our furniture from storage. Two weeks later, our airfreight arrived with the personal items we didn't need while we traveled.

Our treasures from Kabul, handcrafted rosewood furniture, Afghan carpets, made their way by Painted Truck through the Khyber Pass to Karachi, Pakistan. These elaborate lorries, ubiquitous in the region, consisted of dangling hammered metal, bright colored paints, mosaic designs. Truck owners displayed their wealth, religious beliefs, social attitudes on these one-of-a-kind works of pop art. One week after we left Kabul, a freighter from Karachi transported our crated furnishings across the Indian and Pacific Oceans to the Port of Los Angeles, arrived three weeks later.

At age fifty-one, Dad, an experienced professional, knew the world of education, how to inspire others. He knew kids started out in school eager to learn, only to have poverty and gangs destroy their ambitions. He thought about his own constructive influences from Council House in St. Louis, which helped him initiate strategies to assist students in the community.

First, he approached local church leaders to open their churches for after school programs, but they offered little to support this effort. Children as young as first grade affiliated themselves with gangs through older siblings. The school hired terrific teachers, both black and white. They worked hard to sustain enthusiasm toward learning in their students.

In 1975, his first year at Normandie, Dad reconnected with an innovative computer software company he became familiar with before Kabul. He purchased a special computerized reading program with Title I funds, made suggestions to the company to enhance the Language Arts program. Dad set up the new computer lab, hired a computer teacher, made Normandie the first school in LAUSD with a computer lab for students.

All classes rotated into the computer lab, the "hot ticket" for students, each week. The novelty of reading on the computer motivated students. Reading scores increased after the first year.

Dad wanted to involve the community, but most parents struggled to pay rent, put food on the table, many of them single mothers on welfare who didn't do well in school themselves. Parents often didn't emphasize education at home.

The previous principal organized a girls' drill team, directed by a teacher who served in a famous junior college drill team in Texas. An excellent teacher, she demanded great effort, discipline, a positive attitude from her dancers. Girls participated on the team both in school and in the neighborhood.

Then a talented fifth grader named Paul came to Dad's office to ask permission to create a drum corps. Dad loved his idea, purchased the drums and uniforms with Title I funds. After months of practice, the city parade organizers invited the Normandie Elementary School Drill Team and Drum Corps to march in the city parade. More parades followed for this talented group of girls and boys. They won numerous awards and built school pride.

Since many new kindergarteners didn't know their full name and address, Dad made learning this information a priority for all kindergarteners in the first two weeks of school. While he roamed the playground at recess, my father asked random youngsters their names and addresses. They beamed with confidence, recounted their personal information. This impressed Dad. He knew if they learned this, they'd learn to read, write, comprehend math.

Dad worked at Normandie Elementary for three years before he transferred to Dixie Canyon Elementary in Sherman Oaks, cut his commute in half, gave him more time with Mom.

Dad also reengaged with tennis, popular in Southern California, on weekends when the game fit into his busy schedule. Since courts at California State University Northridge (CSUN) filled fast, my father got together with several of his tennis buddies to build their own court to ensure they never again waited for one.

The tennis group found a one-acre lot with a small home for sale one mile from our house, zoned for horse stables. Dad and nine partners purchased the land, renovated the house, rented the building. The rental income paid for an expert contractor who produced a first-class tennis court like a country club. The 10-foot woven hunter green fence provided a windscreen on breezy days. Over time, they added lights for evening games, patio furniture with an umbrella, installed a telephone and refrigerated drinking fountain.

Whenever I broke away from my studies and part-time job, Dad and I played together. He placed the ball in such a precise manner, forced me with each swing to run from one side of the court to the other. He beat me every game.

Dixie Canyon Elementary, a wealthy area like Encino, produced new challenges for Dad and his teachers. The school participated in the forced integration program. The district bused students twenty-five miles to Downtown LA, bused students from Korea Town to Dixie Canyon in a triangular exchange with a third school. Mothers protective of their children traveling far from home, opposed the plans.

Although a district mandate, Dad's personal views on integration did not match Board of Education policy. To bus children twenty to thirty miles from their homes disrupted rather than benefitted learning. Integration carried out this way gave the impression students only learned if they sat next to white children. Dad's experience proved the theory false.

In the early spring of 1980, my father received a call about possible work in Lesotho, a poor, tiny, independent African nation near South Africa. Without hesitation, Dad turned down the Lesotho offer based on its geographic location because continuous violence disrupted South Africa due its apartheid policies. He didn't want to risk his family near a civil war.

Toward the end of his second year at Dixie Canyon Elementary, Dad pondered retirement. After he devoted twenty-nine years to education, he wanted time off in summer to strategize his options. Then a call came to offer him another overseas position.

23

WORKING IN THE WILD

Dad's friend and colleague Tony Lanza, who headed all educational projects for USAID in Afghanistan, submitted my father's name to develop a program to teach English in Africa. Since Dad and Tony continued their friendship by mail, Tony thought Dad a perfect candidate for the job. By early summer, the Lesotho project moved to Kenya because the educational system in East Africa offered more promise for this new form of learning. The Academy for Educational Development (AED) hired Dad to create a unique program to teach children over the radio to speak, read, and write English.

My father married a brave lioness, because Mom followed him everywhere his career took him. In late August 1980, my parents rented out the house in Northridge again, left for their temporary home in Nairobi, Kenya. Rather than retire, Dad took a two-year leave of absence from Los Angeles Unified School District. This gave him time to contemplate his next move in life.

On the way to Nairobi, Dad seized a rare opportunity, took Mom to Greece for five fun-filled days. They toured the Parthenon, the Acropolis, other ancient sites near Athens. They treated their palates to spicy lamb and *dolmas* (stuffed grape leaves) in the *Plaka* (town square) along with other globetrotting tourists. Under the summer stars, they learned traditional Greek dancing while they sipped *ouzo* (licorice liqueur) with friendly locals. They walked hand in hand on the seashore, listened to the tranquil waves of turquoise waters in the Aegean Sea, shared their goals for their next adventure, Nairobi, Kenya.

My parents, bleary-eyed after the all-night flight from Athens, perked up when the plane descended into Nairobi. The pilot swooped down over the golden grasslands of the Serengeti Plains, scattered a herd of gazelle like the wind.

A Kenyan member of the AED team greeted them at the airport at dawn, before the stifling heat of the day took over. She chatted in Kenyan English all the way to the Pan African Hotel, where Mom and Dad first stayed.

After a cool shower followed by a hearty breakfast, they took a taxi to pick up the automobile AED pre-ordered for Dad. In his first attempt to drive on the left side of the road, he realized he wasn't in California any more. In Nairobi, no lines marked individual lanes on the roads, nor did drivers signal when they moved from one lane to another. He felt like Mario Andretti on the speedway, dodged to avoid other cars.

Two years earlier, Kenya's first president, Jomo Kenyatta, died. His presidency recognized the importance of education for a new free nation like Kenya. His first budget allocated more than fifty percent of its funds to education. He insisted they teach English in elementary schools. At age eleven, children took a high school entrance exam in English to determine if they qualified for higher education.

After ten years of freedom from Britain, Kenyan officials knew many children who lived in the bush could not pass the high school entrance exam. When they investigated, they discovered most elementary teachers knew little English themselves. The education authorities approached USAID for help.

When Dad flew to the USAID office in Washington, D.C. for his interview, the officials boasted about an earlier successful mathematics project in Nicaragua, run by Stanford University, where teachers taught lessons via the radio. Then, later in 1983 the leftist Sandinista government came to power, abolished the program.

USAID asked my father, "Why not teach oral and written English over the radio?" Nobody ever attempted this approach before. Washington officials offered Dad the director's post, which required a six-year commitment in Kenya. Although flattered, Dad turned them down, but agreed to a two-year contract to write the initial program.

The AED project worked out of the official Language Institute of Kenya, managed by a pleasant English chap who lived many years in the country, and a Kenyan, Julia, the executive secretary of AED. Since Dad arrived from outside the country before the rest of the team, he and Julia became instant comrades.

Julia's husband directed a sugar cooperative. He also sat in Parliament. Information Julia divulged about Kenya, her ambitions for herself, her family, inspired Dad.

Julia told an interesting story about her grandfather, a chief of the Luo Tribe. For centuries, the animist Luo Tribe worshipped animals and plants. Over the years, her grandfather took three wives, a custom allowed to any man able to pay the dowries. When his youngest wife became ill, Julia's grandfather turned to missionaries in the area for help. The doctor at the Seventh Day Adventist Church visited the tribe every day to administer medication, which healed her. Impressed with the doctor's healing methods, the chief converted the entire tribe to Christianity.

Dad found no personal typewriters in the office, asked Julia for permission to use her typewriter to write a letter home.

Julia grabbed her steno pad. "Go ahead, dictate the letter. I want to practice my shorthand, then I'll type up the letter."

Minutes later, Julia presented the typed letter to Dad. When my father laughed, Julia's smile drooped. "Why are you amused?" she asked.

He said, "You spelled several of the words in the British manner.

"I'll retype the letter."

"No, no, since I'm in a British-English-speaking country, my friends and family will enjoy the letter with British spelling."

They both laughed. This cemented a wonderful friendship between them.

It took weeks to get the AED project organized. Although Dad masked his emotions well, the inexperience of the other team members frustrated him. Of the four American members, only Dad brought actual teaching experience. Two of the men held recent PhDs, the only woman worked at the Smithsonian Institution in Washington, D.C. AED also hired three native Kenyans with teaching experience, one man from the Luo tribe, two women from the Kikuyu tribe. One of the Kenyan women with radio experience took responsibility to tape the lessons. She interviewed Kenyan actors to read the scripts to help the children learn Kenyan English.

After two months of procrastination and bickering, the team made headway. They settled on simple core principles. Young children had short attention spans. Therefore, they kept the teaching segments short, no longer than two minutes for each new concept. They decided to teach through songs, copied *Sesame Street*, a children's show phenomenon in the United States. The project required the vocabulary to match the official first grade readers. Each core sentence such as, "I am a ... boy," used a boy's voice, then "I am a ... girl," used a girl's voice. Once introduced, a core sentence used only one new phrase at a time. The team broadcast new phrases daily for two weeks then reviewed them again four weeks later.

Dad shortened the review segments to forty-five seconds each, instead of two minutes. Each full lesson lasted no more than twenty-eight minutes to allow for advertisements before and after each lesson. The Voice of Kenya Radio regulated this short amount of airtime. Dad knew the plan allowed too little time to accomplish the goals, but he made the most of each minute.

Each team member settled into his or her area of expertise. Dad wrote the segments to teach spoken and written English. A Kenyan wrote the radio instructions for the teachers and students. One of the Americans researched possible teaching approaches. The former Smithsonian member wrote catchy ditties with demonstrative words.

Kenya's school year began in January, after its rainy season. Moderate temperatures prevailed, food became more abundant, allowed students more time to study. The AED team taped the first lessons a month before the January start of school, maintained a one-month lead time throughout the school year.

Since most schools in the bush had no electricity, AED hired a young Kenyan, George, to deliver battery-operated radios to seven experimental schools scattered across the country. Kenya's size, double the size of Nevada, meant George needed about five weeks to deliver the radios.

They needed to replace the radios because of theft or breakage. One principal valued his replaced radio, took it home each night after thieves stole the first one from the school building.

From time to time, George also delivered written instructions to the teachers. Rutted dirt roads, flash floods in the rainy season, ambushes on the roads caused schools to go without radio transmissions for weeks at a time.

Each day, on completion of their chores, children in the bush gathered around their teacher for the anticipated English lesson. A crowd assembled in huts of mud and straw, while a few met in small cement classroom structures. No screens or glass covered the open windows of these barren concrete buildings. Students and teachers welcomed the warm breezes from the amber plains.

Children of all ages, eager to learn, sat cross-legged on the hard reddish-dirt floor. A few of the wealthy tribes made woven rugs or tanned zebra or lion skin for the classroom floor.

Most teachers sat on primitive stools made of a simple animal hide secured to the top of three whittled tree branches. The branches held the seat, formed a tripod.

The children listened to each broadcast with all eyes glued to the tiny electronic box which transmitted voices in English. The children, ages six through eleven, repeated phrases, sang songs, mimicked the English voices broadcast on the radio while they swatted the occasional fly or insect off their half-naked bodies.

After the program aired its first month of lessons on the Voice of Kenya Radio, Mom observed the results in action at a market in Nairobi. While she walked to her car in the parking lot, she heard attendants sing the learning songs, repeat the English phrases. Kenya, with only one radio station controlled by the government, commanded a captive audience. Dad enjoyed her story at a quiet dinner at home.

English lessons became a part of Kenyan pop culture, like catchy commercial jingles in the United States. Children and adults sang the songs together. Whether they lived in the bush or in the cities, Kenyans learned to speak, read, write English via the radio.

Dad planned most of his lessons while he drove to the office. Often, he witnessed wild monkeys frolic along the roadside with each other like children. This sparked more ideas about animal sounds, behaviors.

In June, the sixth month of school, the team ran an interest survey at various schools scattered among seven different tribes. They played a tape of animal sounds from the Smithsonian Institution at each pilot school. Farm animals and wild animals seen in Kenya chattered on the tape. Most students did not recognize the sounds of the animals.

Through tribal customs, Kenyan children saw animals in a different way than we did. They knew elephants trampled their *shamba* (farmlands), diminished their food supply. Lions wandered into their camps, mauled or ate members of their tribe. Most children in Western nations loved to hear songs about animals. Not in Kenya. Ancestral traditions imbued most Kenyan children with a respectful fear of animals. Because of their survival instinct, this fear became stronger among those who lived in the bush.

For two reasons, Dad began with songs like *Old McDonald Had a Farm* and *Ten Little Monkeys Jumping on the Bed* to introduce animal behavior. These songs, which depicted tame animals, not violent toward humans, encouraged students to repeat English language words.

At work, Dad edited lesson details, wrote effective, entertaining dialogues, developed all-inclusive repetitive lessons cumulative in nature. Each segment became a foundation for the next, building vocabulary for comprehensive learning. Most of his material came from his prior experience with early childhood curriculum for the County of Los Angeles.

Based on his experience teaching English as a Second Language (ESL) to Khan and Ali in Kabul, Dad used commands with actions in many of the lessons. His right hand often ached while he wrote his material by hand.

After the first year, the AED team developed a universal English skills test to evaluate students' progress in each of the pilot schools. The results astounded them. At first, the team thought they made a calculation error, yet after they rechecked the scores, found them conclusive. Overall English proficiency improved by fifty-four percent nationwide. My father celebrated. His work proved successful, he felt gratified.

In the second year of the AED project, the greatest challenge became to keep the attention of children. Many contended with the equatorial weather, impoverished lifestyles. In the rainy season, a tough time for those in the bush, the hunt for food proved difficult because many wild animals didn't migrate then. A few tribes placed education lower on the priority scale because they fought for daily sustenance.

Dad continued to write more fun, interesting scripts. The more curricula my father wrote, the easier the words flowed.

The AED team gelled, let go of their differences to focus on their team goal, to help Kenyans gain fluency in English, provide a constant stream of English instruction broadcast on the Voice of Kenya Radio for all students to learn.

The fun came when the AED team visited pilot schools around the country. George drove the van for all four members of the writing team.

He stayed on the main highway, but many schools located in the bush forced them to drive on unpaved roads the color of bricks.

On one trip, when Dad turned to look out the rear window, he saw clouds of red sand behind them, stirred up by the official van. The natural beauty mesmerized him. On long drives, they peered out the windows for more than an hour at a time in hypnotic silence.

Whenever possible, George, proud of his native land, navigated past wildlife in its natural habitat. Dad called this the highlight of each trip. One early morning, they found a herd of five giraffe stretching their long necks to munch the leafy treetops of an acacia tree. Their frail legs carried a strong upper body, elongated neck, head up to the umbrella shaped tree.

George turned off the engine, coasted the van to a few feet away from the herd. Everyone in the van froze. Dad noted each giraffe wore a unique brown and white stenciled pattern. To avoid startling the beautiful creatures, they spoke in whispered voices inside the van, snapped silent photos.

Dad's thoughts drifted to an article he read about giraffes. Not only do they use their six-foot long necks to eat in high places, they also search for predators like a periscope on a submarine. Dad saw one reach around to scratch his butt with his mouth. An adult giraffe consumes up to 140 pounds of vegetation per day, spends fifteen to twenty hours of each day foraging for food. To stay hydrated in the hot Savannah, the giraffe drinks ten to twelve gallons of water at a time in the dry season when water holes tend to dry up.

One of the women mumbled a few words, snapped him back into focus. Dad studied the giraffe a few feet from the van. Although conscious of the intrusion, the magnificent stilted animal continued to chew in its grinding motion. One mother brought a mouthful of greens to her calf, too short to reach the delicate leaves at the top of the tree. Then both mother and calf wiggled their ears like little propellers on a toy airplane. Dad grinned at the endearing encounter.

Another time they stopped to watch three lions attack a herd of zebra. Dad lifted his binoculars, focused the lenses on the short stretch of greenery George pointed out in the distance. From under a bush, all three lions darted like missiles toward the striped creatures. Caught off guard, the flock of zebras ran in all directions. With its sharp teeth, one male lion grabbed the leg of a young zebra. The other two female lions retreated. Their meal awaited them. The zebra squirmed, cried out, but too late. All three lions ate its flesh.

Gruesome or not, Dad loved the call of the wild. In Kenya, nature came to life like Rudyard Kipling's stories in *The Jungle Book*. To witness the survival of the fittest among animals in their natural habitat inspired Dad because it depicted the circle of life.

Later, when he arrived at the designated school, Dad discovered a creative teacher used innovative methods to reinforce the English lessons. She made signs from used cardboard, hung them around the necks of selected students who played the role of each character in the prior radio lesson. The students beamed like stars in a Hollywood movie, recited the English scripts. This class reviewed daily, to make each lesson come to life for them.

From then on, all teachers used this technique. They rotated students to act out the scripts to develop strong self-confidence in both the English language and the students. Children studied with more diligence because they knew their turns to perform approached.

In the first year, various Kenyan government officials expressed concern about the AED project's merit. However, after they saw the positive results in classrooms and the scores on paper, the animosity faded. The Director of Education in Kenya also conveyed his sincere compliments to the AED team, which made my father proud.

In the middle of the second year, the woman who worked at the Smithsonian Institution left the project early to return to Washington, D.C. Dad, relieved, thought her a pain to work with. To replace her, AED hired a young man who worked for the Peace Corps in Ecuador. Dad respected him because he brought creative song ideas to the project, accepted suggestions, kept his ego in check.

One month before my father's departure from Kenya, AED hired an independent company from Egypt to run comprehensive assessments in the seven pilot schools, the ultimate test from this unbiased Egyptian company.

The company tallied the scores, again the evaluation showed impressive results, a fifty-nine percent increase in overall literacy in the English language throughout the country. They tested more than seven tribes in the pilot schools, demonstrated all students learned the same.

Although at times, his interaction with colleagues frustrated him, to meet the assignment objectives pleased Dad. Despite what others on the team did, my father remained committed to the advancement of the team's goal: teach English to all school-aged Kenyans. Gratified, Dad left Kenya with a solid program to teach English to the next generation, satisfied the project would flourish long after his departure from the Academy for Educational Development. His work changed lives, transformed a nation.

24

SAFARI LIVING

At the Pan African Hotel, Dad rented a temporary three-room apartment. Mom and Dad registered at the American Embassy, located Dottie, a nurse who worked in Kabul, moved to Nairobi. She loved to hear from my parents, insisted they come to dinner.

Over the next weeks, Dottie invited my parents to numerous diplomatic events where they made friends with embassy employees from around the world. Dad kept up on current affairs, became a source for events around the world.

In the first few months, my father met countless long-time British citizens of Kenya. Some knew their ancestry back to the colonization of Kenya at the turn of the twentieth century. My parents attended the theatre, restaurants, nightclubs. They celebrated their first Thanksgiving in Kenya crammed into the tiny apartment. Yet they acclimated. Apartment living allowed Mom to meet several English wives who also lived at the hotel. They showed her scores of cool spots in Nairobi, among them the Nairobi Game Park outside the city.

At the hotel, my parents became best friends with the Chapmans, a charming English couple, refugees, forced to leave Uganda when the civil war broke out. Don and Pat met, married, raised their family in Kenya. Don was Director of British Oxygen in Uganda until Idi Amin began one of the worst genocides in the twentieth century. Dad found the Chapmans delightful, worldly people.

While Dad worked hard, Mom explored marketplaces, attended luncheons with other international wives, looked for a home to rent. A portion of Dad's benefits package from AED included a generous housing allowance, which meant they did not need to live in the hotel for two years. Prior to Thanksgiving, Mom found a spectacular home for rent in a beautiful residential neighborhood of Nairobi.

The green lawn edged a curved concrete driveway large enough for six cars to park, reminded her of Encino in the 1960's. Most homes she looked at in the city had no electric air conditioner. Mom appreciated the sprawling brownii trees in front of the house, noting they became excellent cooling agents during the hot days.

The landlord showed Mom around, but she hesitated to rent to Americans. Mom said, "I want you to meet my husband before you decide."

Mom picked Dad up at his office in their white four-door Peugeot, drove to the home, a ten-minute ride through a luscious tree-covered greenbelt in Nairobi.

When they arrived at the house, Dad noticed the polished white Range Rover parked in the driveway. An attractive, well-dressed woman welcomed them with pleasantries. Inside the tri-level *nyumba* (house), Dad understood why Mom fell in love with the place.

A profusion of light poured in through the floor to ceiling picture windows at the back of the home. The cluster of colorful rose bushes in full bloom on a canvas of plush green lawn in the back yard awed Dad. Dark ebony-wood floors covered every level, added a rich organic spice to the home. The elegant entry level flowed right, led down the hallway to three spacious bedrooms, two full bathrooms.

After five minutes of polite banter, Dad discovered the property owner married the alcoholic brother of the late President Jomo Kenyatta, his third wife, intelligent, powerful in the family. With her Kenyatta money, she purchased coffee plantations, a chain of shoe stores, wheat farms, which, combined, provided a substantial income for each of her brothers. Dad employed his diplomatic skills, made her an ally, signed the lease to this one-of-a-kind home, planned their move for right after Thanksgiving.

Weeks earlier, Mom and Dad received a letter from Tony and Camille Lanza, friends from Kabul now in Virginia, who wrote they planned to travel to Kenya on business, wanted to spend Thanksgiving with the Cutlers. Dad and Mom were overjoyed such faithful friends wanted to visit them on another continent. Dottie ordered the turkey. Mom prepared the bird like always, with bread stuffing, fresh herbs, butter, other delectable items.

Top left, Faye, Alex, and Ruth; Center, Morrie, Alex, Ruth, Bottom, Masai Mara Tribe

The seven urbane companions, all well-traveled, intelligent, compassionate people created a progressive dinner, began with drinks, moved to appetizers upstairs in the Chapmans' apartment, moved downstairs to my parents' place for the meal. The conversations ranged around the globe, each funny, fabulous story topped the one before. In the small sitting room with this enlightened group of dear friends, Dad chuckled to himself. He thought of his first Thanksgiving in St. Louis, when his mother made a goose instead of a turkey. Dad called their first Thanksgiving in Nairobi one of the best, he gave thanks to live such a full, joyous life.

On weekends, my parents took long drives with new friends like the Chapmans to local animal parks. Over seventy-five percent of Kenya consisted of government preserved nature parks patrolled by game wardens, many less than a day's drive from Nairobi. Often, they brought gourmet picnic lunches prepared by their cook Ndui, other times they dined at the safari game park restaurants.

Most game park restaurants served an exquisite luncheon on open-air, wood-covered patios for safari goers, presented in fine British fashion with crisp, white linens. Casablanca fans stirred the warm Kenyan air. The group sipped iced tea to quench their parched mouths after the long drive through the Serengeti Plains. Dad kept his eye on the water hole adjacent to every safari lodge, hoped to catch a glimpse of a warthog, wildebeest, or a herd of elephants.

These early experiences in Kenya proved helpful when family and friends from the United States came to visit them in Kenya. Mom counted twenty-one sets of visitors in the two years, among them Terri and I on separate visits, in stark contrast to no visitors in Afghanistan. With a multitude of guests, Mom and Dad went on Safari two to three weekends a month over the two-year period. They called their African home "The Cutler Hilton."

They joined one of several country clubs in Nairobi, where Dad played tennis, made new friends. One young couple, Biff, the marketing manager for Caltex, the Standard Oil Company outside the United States, and his wife, the Director of Nursing in one of the hospitals, "adopted" them. Whenever Caltex hosted parties, they included my parents. The CEO of Caltex welcomed their presence.

Biff offered to teach Dad the game of squash, which he never played before. Biff won the first game, but never won again the entire two years they lived in Kenya. Between sets, Dad bonded with Biff, shared stories of their U.S. Air Force days. Biff, a Gunnery Sergeant in the Korean War, flew B-52s. After games, Biff bemoaned his plight for everyone to hear, paid for the first round of drinks.

Dad kidded Biff. "I always win because a Lieutenant Colonel ranks above a peasant sergeant."

They laughed at this special joke like schoolboys.

Dad socialized with friends to balance work and leisure. Yet he and Mom missed their two daughters. Our parents wanted both my sister Terri and me to visit. Terri regretted not visiting during Dad's two-year contract in Afghanistan, agreed to travel to Kenya in September of 1981.

25

VISITING DAD

Although we communicated by mail via the diplomatic pouch, the letters took ten to twelve days each way, left many items unsaid. The first week of June 1981, I jetted off to Kenya to reunite with my parents.

When I stepped into the foyer of their East African home, tears welled up in my eyes. In my heart, I felt the same warmth when I read letters from them, realized how much I missed my parents. Even 9,600 miles from California, I felt at home in Nairobi with Mom and Dad.

Ndui, their cook, emerged from the kitchen, wore a big white smile above a pristine apron the color of his teeth. He greeted me like an honored guest. Sweet aromas floated down from the upper level kitchen. Dad said, "We told Ndui how much you loved sweets. He baked a special cake in your honor."

Morrie and Diane

They asked if I wanted to rest. Although exhausted, I was too amped up to sleep. Mom and I unpacked my luggage. One suitcase contained clothes for four weeks, the other American goodies for my parents. I brought See's candy, kosher salamis, jellybeans, Red Vines, with a few unmentionables Mom needed. Although we could purchase them in Nairobi, imported items cost outrageous amounts. Dad grabbed one of the five-pound salamis, retreated to the kitchen.

A few minutes later, he returned with a small plate piled high with thin-sliced salami, which he offered to us. He flashed a satisfied smile. Neither Mom nor I took a slice when we saw how much Dad enjoyed this Jewish delicacy.

Mom wanted to show me around town. After I ate the light snack Ndui prepared for me, Dad said he wanted us to drop him off at his office while Mom took me shopping in downtown Nairobi.

I'm not sure what I expected, perhaps a more primitive, tribal environment. Hotels, restaurants, stores along the street showcased the latest European fashions, culinary wares. We bought two dozen fresh-cut roses from a street vendor for twenty Kenyan shillings, less than two American dollars. Mom wanted them for Dottie, who hosted a dinner for me in the evening. Then she looped her arm around mine while we crossed the street, said, "Follow me."

I ran to keep up with her until we stopped on the next corner. She pointed to a man who swept up thousands of dead beetles across the road. To step on them sounded like a walkthrough broken glass. Creepy, but I reminded myself, characteristic of Africa. Without another word, Mom smiled, motioned me to follow. I trailed behind her, tried to figure out our destination. A couple of blocks later, we stopped in front of an exquisite white building with black and white striped awning. The storefront displayed mounds of candy, each tucked into tiny white accordion papers.

We stepped into the immaculate candy store. Glossy black and white checkerboard tiles lined the floor, a perfect replica of See's Candies back home. Mom spoiled me because she knew how much I loved chocolate. My mouth watered from the sweet aromas. Not a fingerprint showed on the pristine glass displays filled with candies of every variety.

Mom encouraged me to choose the goodie I wanted. My eyes surveyed the enormous selection. "Look closer," she said.

My eyes widened. An *insect* candy store. We both ran out of the store like two schoolgirls. Mom told me Kenyans considered insects a delicacy. This store offered the customary milk chocolate, semi-sweet, dark, white chocolate, all covered beetles. Additional culinary delights included glazed, sugar-coated, honey-coated scorpions, ants, grasshoppers, worms. We giggled the rest of the afternoon. Mom told me she did the same thing to Dad after she discovered the insect candy shop.

On the way to Dottie's for dinner, I told the story to Dad. He chuckled, said, "Looks deceive in a culture like Kenya."

Two days later, we departed on an eight-day safari Dad planned. In Swahili the word *safari* means journey. The first day we drove 160 kilometers (about 100 miles) under a canopy of azure-blue sky. Our excitement grew each time we spotted herds of moose-like wildebeests near wild buffalo, whose horns grew down into flip hairdos, out at the horizon. A while later, we saw a small pack of hyenas attack the remains of a previous kill. To see the open red flesh of a gazelle grossed us out, yet to play in the wild with these amazing creatures exhilarated us.

The color of the red soil deepened near Amboseli National Park, located at the southeastern edge of Kenya. I understood why Dad tied hefty black trash bags around our suitcases before he loaded them in the trunk. While the car protected the luggage, dense red dust settled inside everything. Near the park, a few giant anthills appeared on both sides of the road. Within the next kilometer, hundreds of five- to six-foot anthills lined the road. When I said the scene reminded me of the old Hollywood cowboy and Indian movies where the Apaches staked cowboys to an anthill to die, Dad and Mom chuckled in agreement.

Our rooms opened onto a view of the greatest wilderness landscape on Earth. Amboseli served as a sanctuary for thousands of different species. Tall green acacia trees sprouted up like stalks of broccoli across miles of golden grasslands. The classic stone-built lodge overlooked a natural waterhole where big game, like elephants, rhinos, lions stopped to drink. Because of the endless underground water supply, hundreds of varieties of wildlife trek to Amboseli each year. Dad's favorites? Red Elephants, found no other place on earth. Okay, not born red.

Dad explained, "Fine red volcanic soil coats their hides."

After we unpacked, Dad said, "Always draw the white mosquito net around the bed at night to avoid the way Mom looked in Machu Picchu."

We smiled at each other at the memory of Mom covered with more than thirty mosquito bites, instead of the three or four bites on Dad and me. She had an allergic reaction to the bites. We called in a Peruvian doctor, who gave her an antihistamine to calm the lesions. I'm not sure Mom liked her role of brunt of the joke, but this established Dad's point to use the mosquito nets.

From the open-air patio at lunch, we observed the colossal Mount Kilimanjaro in nearby Tanzania. Although the base of this impressive mountain lay forty miles away, no fence separated the two countries. It looked close enough to touch its hardened black molten rock from the veranda ... surreal. We dined at a rustic, upscale Kenyan resort, looked at the tallest mountain in Africa, across the Tanzanian border.

Dad said, "Mount Kilimanjaro, the tallest free-standing mountain on earth, inspires a majestic appeal unlike Mount Everest in Nepal, part of the Himalayan mountain range." Both Dad and I thought the mountain an awesome sight.

A natural environment surrounded the lodge. No loud music, voices or televised football games disrupted nature's tranquility.

On our walk after lunch, we stayed on the posted paths. Armed rangers strolled the grounds to protect guests from vicious intruders. In the trees we saw birds of every color of the rainbow harmonize with sweet songs. Farther down, we came across a family of bare butt baboons, not their official name, the one we settled on because of the thick black hair everywhere on their bodies except their bare butts. The two adorable babies swung through the trees like Olympic gymnasts. Dad pointed out a female, who groomed the large alpha male, picked insects off his back, ate them. He joked, "Baboons get it right. The female treats her mate with dignity." Mom and I ignored him, left Dad behind on the scenic tree-covered path.

Dinner seemed like an afterthought while we watched the wildlife drink from the waterhole under the stars. A couple of warthogs waddled up before dusk. With their dirty tusks above decayed teeth, they looked like scruffy, bad-boy cartoon images of our American hogs.

"After the daytime heat cools, the animals hunt for food and water," Dad whispered. "The waterhole lures them in like bees to honey."

When we glanced up between mouthfuls, we watched elegant impala, deer-like animals, a sleek black jaguar with glittery eyes quench their thirst. One lonesome zebra strayed to the water hole alone.

While we waited for dessert, a gargantuan male elephant appeared. Everyone in the open dining area looked up. When he flapped his huge fan-like ears, we felt the breeze. Then he lifted his trunk, sounded his bugle, announced to his herd they could drink. Within minutes, over forty elephants of all sizes moved into sight around the giant waterhole. Many of us stood at the lodge rail, no more than eight feet from these mammoth herbivores.

Dad detected fear in my expression, reminded me, "Although these elephants could stampede all of us, they only attack when a stranger threatens their young or they're hungry. Since elephants only eat vegetation, we're safe."

The next morning. My father said, "Remember how Mowgli, the boy raised by wolves in Kipling's tale *The Jungle Book*, turned every stroll into an adventure?"

We set out early for the nearby game park, Tsavo West, to beat the heat. Dad called Tsavo West an ecological masterpiece, with an endless underground water supply filtered through thousands of feet of volcanic rock from Mount Kilimanjaro's ice cap runoff.

Thompson gazelle frolicked like stage dancers across the open Serengeti plains. Dad thought the long white stripes painted down their backs resembled those of skunks. We all agreed their unusual markings set them apart from other breeds of gazelle we saw.

Except for an occasional vehicle in the other lane, we drove the two-lane highway alone. I glanced out the side window when the car slowed.

Mom sat up, said, "Black rhino!"

I saw one solitary rhino mosey across the road like on a Sunday stroll. "Black rhino," Dad said. He nodded at the pointed hook-lipped mouth. "Larger, more square face than on white and grey rhino."

The rhino's wrinkled skin made him look old, but all rhino get wrinkles. Dad slowed to a stop. "Black rhino, rare in Kenya, almost extinct around the world."

Mom said, "Quite a find on our safari."

The rhino stopped, his wide body stretched across the middle of the road. He turned his head, looked straight at us with fierce black eyes.

"Looks like he's fought a few battles," Dad said. I noticed the jagged scars on his dark torso.

Dad kept his foot on the brake while he made sure the car sat ten feet away from the beast. “Rhino often charge cars without warning,” he said. “They’re close to extinct because poachers kill rhino for their horns. They sell them for a high price on the black market, because it’s believed to offer aphrodisiac properties.”

I said, “Rhino never walk backward, they only move in a forward direction.” I felt good when both my parents said they didn’t know the trivia. After he idled a few minutes, the rhino moved on. We did too.

The highway led us into Ngulia Hills, the lower extension of Mount Kilimanjaro. Lush green hillsides draped the black volcanic mountain. Dad parked, we exited the car. We breathed in the fresh clean air, stood at the ridge of the road for minutes, in utter silence. Dad said, “Without a doubt, this is one of the most exquisite views in all of Kenya.”

After we lunched at the Ngulia Lodge, we drove a short distance to Mzima Springs, a sanctuary which attracted a profusion of wildlife. Hundreds of varieties of palms lined the banks of the river like skyscrapers in New York City. Dad shielded his eyes from the intense sun, pointed up at the 40-foot tall red-stemmed fronds. “Kenya exports rope, twine from these raffia palms to many parts of the world,” he said. “The lower parts of the leaves on the raffia palms build up a wax used for floor and shoe polish.”

The springs, a lush tropical oasis, teemed with colorful fish, birds, crocodiles, hippos. We gazed into the slow flow of the transparent blue-green water, watched marble-eyed crocodiles prey on innocent fish. A few hippos floated on the water, twirled their tiny ears like propellers on toy planes ready for takeoff. These massive submarines cast a brownish tone from their skin, while the smaller ones radiated a purple tint in the sunlight. Park rangers with rifles marched along the dirt path to a bridge. We all felt more secure to know they protected us from savage wildlife.

At the end of the bridge lay a traditional tiki hut constructed of dried palms. Uneven rock steps led down into cool subterranean shade. We all grinned with a sigh of relief at the cooler temperature, realized we stumbled on a primitive version of an underwater view tank.

A large glass window five feet wide by four feet high revealed the underwater world of Mzima Springs. We squished our bottoms together on a natural carved stone bench inside the hut.

Dad said, "Feels like an episode of Jacques Cousteau."

Through the translucent water, we observed buoyant hippos. Their tubular bodies danced in slow motion like oversized ballerinas. All shapes, sizes, colors of fish glided into view. We enjoyed the show.

Dad shared the pyramid of life in Mzima Springs. "On cool nights, the hippos graze on the nearby grasslands, later they deposit copious amounts of dung into the stream. The dung provides a place for insects to hide, food for snails and fish." Dad added, "The algae form on hippo's thick skin, nourish turtles, fish, scorpions."

Dad, like a scientific tour guide, explained the natural food chain. "In daylight, the transparent purity of Mzina's calm pools permits fish to avoid crocodiles. However, at night crocs lie with mouths agape, slam their jaws on any fish who swims too close."

A giant kingfisher bird scooped its large beak into the water, grabbed an eight-inch carp. Freaked us out, but what a treasured memory to see the cycle of life below the surface of the water.

In the morning, we left on our next adventure, to Mombasa, a splendid city by the sea. We loved the tranquil resort in Mombasa, a tropical paradise, tall coconut palms waved in the light breeze, fine white sand draped the shore, a superb coral reef attracted the most colorful sea life.

This international port appealed to many people, British sailors, Europeans on holiday, the Zimbabwean Judo Team in town for a match. The blend of people who visited the resort fascinated Dad. He made friends with everyone within his "three-foot rule."

After we cooled off in the crystal blue pool, Dad told stories of Mombasa's rich history to Mom and me. "Portuguese explorers, the first known European visitors to this paradise on the Indian Ocean, encountered Shafi'i Muslins, who ruled the island for centuries. These religious, trustworthy, righteous people lived in harmony until Mombasa became the center of trade for spices, gold, and ivory in the early nineteenth century."

I asked Dad about the slave trade out of Africa.

"Most took place on the Ivory Coast in Northwestern Africa," he said. "In the late 1800's, the Shafi'i Muslims granted this port to the British government, which made Mombasa the trade capital of the British East Africa Protectorate, that built railroads, bridges." Dad sipped his iced tea, reminded us, "Kenya reclaimed this land when they declared their independence from Britain in 1963."

At the resort, Dad and I swam in the warm Indian Ocean, marveled at the vast amount of marine life in the coral reef. Without a mask, the transparent blue water offered ten feet of visibility. Under the water, we saw a tapestry of rainbow-colored coral in whimsical shapes lining the reef. Vibrant fish floated in with the tide. Dad said, "Makes a great movie, I'd title it, *The Wonderful Underwater World of Color*."

We body surfed our way into shore. My thoughts drifted back to the summer of 1964, when Dad took us to Mexico. In the surf at Mazatlan, Wayne and Terri body surfed with Dad, but I, frightened, stayed on the sandy shore with Mom. In my twenties, Dad and I bobbed in the tepid Indian Ocean together, enjoyed the time of our lives.

We lazed around the pool for the remainder of the afternoon. Mom and Dad *kibitzed* (conversed) with other vacationers from around the world, each shared travel stories, sipped umbrella-topped cocktails. Late in the day, the seven members of the Zimbabwean Judo Team, six Caucasian, one dark-skinned, converged in the pool, elated because they won their meet.

We became friends with these polite, refined young gentlemen in their twenties, who asked many questions about the United States.

An hour passed while we talked, swam. I noticed the dark-skinned team member sat off to one side when he left the pool. I motioned for him to sit with us. He shook his head, waved his acknowledgement of my gesture.

Gerald, the team captain, said, "Although he's a valued member of the team, he's not allowed to socialize with us."

My head tilted. His racial attitude stunned me. I asked, "What do you mean he can't socialize with you?"

Gerald said, "Although the government abolished apartheid in Zimbabwe a year ago, the way people think won't change overnight. "Regardless of what he or the other teammates feel, things stay this way for now.

Mom and Dad left the pool area to relax in their room before dinner. I looked forward to further discussion with Dad.

Following breakfast, the next day, while we loaded the car to leave for our last destination, Voi Safari Camp, several members of the Zimbabwean Judo Team said good-bye. After I gave each a friendly hug, I approached the dark-skinned member nearby. Gerald told me he brought a gift for me. He extended his dark hand, unfolded his fingers, revealed a green soapstone carving of a rhino. He told me he made it the night before, because I showed friendship toward him. His gift touched me. Dad called it, "A display of international diplomacy at its best."

It took a little over an hour to reach the hilltop lodge of Voi, built into the mountain in Tsavo East. Like every lodge in Kenya, the view promised spectacular sights of animals in the wild. Our accommodations, sparser than at Amboseli Game Park, possessed only the essentials of a double bed, one small bathroom, no dresser or chair in the room, no pictures on the walls of distressed wood. I felt fortunate to have my own puny bathroom. A small oval mirror hung above the plain white sink with the toilet to the left. A dim light bulb dangled from the ceiling. The shower floor consisted of one-inch square white tiles grouted with burnt-red soil. A simple shower curtain hung in front of the hand-held shower faucet. Mom and Dad's room, identical, in reverse.

After we checked in, we set out for Lugard Falls up the road. We hiked to the top of the dirt path, found the falls, more like a slow river than cascades of water. Crocodiles sunned themselves on the hot boulders. They looked like huge brown prehistoric lizards, the biggest we ever saw. Despite the heat and natural water source, no bugs.

Dad said, "They named Lugard Falls after Sir Frederick Lugard, a British officer who became Governor of Hong Kong, then Governor of Nigeria."

I asked, "Why did Kenyans name the falls after him?"

Dad said, "Lord Lugard developed a scheme to emancipate the slaves from Arabs who controlled parts of Kenya and Uganda in the early 1900s."

We continued to hike, stayed clear of crocodiles, hopped from rock to rock across the river, noticed birds fly from the occasional trees near enormous boulders. Unlike the lava rock, Mzima Springs source, centuries of water flow eroded these smooth stones. We spotted two park rangers along the way. Then a British voice near the top hollered, "Elephants! Come here!" We scurried to the top, made sure to watch out for crocodiles, took care to not slip into the water for fear of crocs under the surface.

On the other side of the open ridge we found an animated pool party. My imagination unleashed itself, conjured up cartoon images of playful elephants with tiny paper party hats on their huge heads. I saw them smile, dance, blow lyrical notes out of their raised trunks. Springbok splashed through the lagoon like choreographed stallions. A couple of buffalo soothed their bodies from the intense heat. All eight of us kept our distance. We found shade, sat our bums on the rocks, enjoyed the performance.

On our way back to the lodge, we saw gazelle in full force on the Serengeti. The safari canvas unfolded under endless blue skies, wildlife frolicked across the golden savannah, unlike anything we ever witnessed. The gazelle looked like graceful dancers, jumped, glided in synchronized movement. Dad said, "They're gorgeous to watch."

After a fun afternoon on safari, we needed cool showers, a relaxed dinner, a good night's rest prior to our journey back to Nairobi.

The next morning, we finished breakfast in the company of an extended family of baboons, comfortable among humans, who begged for food on the patio. Dad handed his partly-eaten slice of toast to a female. She stuffed it into her mouth, moved closer for more. We held onto our purses to keep them safe.

Dad loaded the luggage into the trunk. We set out for the half-day drive home. Forty kilometers down the coast, we stopped at the largest fish merchant in Kenya. Dad seemed to know the owner, a jolly man who gave us a brief tour of his operation. We saw local fishermen dock their boats filled with the day's catch, ready to sell their fish to the seafood company. Dad told me later he wrote a story and several lesson plans around the fishing industry in Kenya based on our visit. Mom and I picked out three huge lobsters for Ndui to cook.

Back in Nairobi several days later, Mom and Dad threw an elegant dinner party in my honor to introduce me to their friends in Nairobi. It felt like my "Coming Out" party. I enjoyed meeting professionals from around the globe with the common interest to improve life for Kenyans.

I watched Dad in his element. He exuded confidence rather than arrogance, debated with top executives and international diplomats. I liked how he played Devil's Advocate to hear their opinions.

He worked hard to write English curriculum for the Kenyan government, yet always left time to sightsee, rest, enjoy others. In addition, Dad received several weeks of paid vacation to use throughout each year, one of the perks of working abroad.

Dad's work kept him challenged. He and Mom engaged with the international community in Nairobi most every day. They seemed content with each other, enjoyed their life in Kenya. They played a great deal since the pay in developing nations like Kenya afforded them a luxurious lifestyle not possible in the U.S. After we shared four weeks of safari adventures, ate delicious food, formed heartfelt memories with my parents, I returned to California.

Morrie and granddaughter Tamara

In September, Terri spent three weeks with Mom and Dad in Kenya. She brought a special present for Dad: his adorable three-year-old granddaughter, Tamara. Terri made sure to pack enough toys, games and Tamara's favorite pink plastic roller skates, which she used in the big curved driveway her first day there.

Days after Terri arrived with Tamara, the Kenyan government invited Dad to watch a baby elephant born in Meru, a rare occasion, since an elephant gestates for twenty-two months. Females seldom give birth in captivity. Dad thought the birth of a baby elephant made a fine story for his lessons.

On the long drive north toward the Ethiopian border, Tamara talked non-stop about the baby elephant. Terri gazed out the car window. "I imagined Kenya much dryer, dustier, like I've seen in the movies," she said.

Dad said, "The recent rainy season makes the bush green. For Kenyans, this happiest time of year creates an abundance of food and water for people and wildlife."

Mom played tour guide while Dad focused on the road. To the left, a dazzle of zebras munched on fresh green grass. Tamara asked to see a lion. With a roar, Dad promised her to find lions while in Kenya. Tamara giggled. Further up the road, a herd of giraffe sprawled across the golden plains. Tamara watched in silence, appreciated the natural beauty of these stunning creatures.

They checked into their rooms in Meru National Park, but no one knew when the birth might happen. A few minutes before midnight, a bell signaled them to come. Dozens of guests ran into the designated area surrounded by foliage. Within minutes, the pink baby elephant, who weighed more than 100 kilos, dropped five feet from its mother's womb, landed on all four feet, like a sturdy pink table. Cheers echoed from the crowd. Then, like thunder from a rain cloud, the other elephants erupted in furious action, threw dirt at the pink baby with their feet and trunks. It seemed abusive. Dad feared a stampede.

One of the officials near Dad set him at ease. "They disguise the baby from predators. The dirt, a natural sunscreen, protects the calf's tender pink skin from the sun's harsh rays."

Seconds later, Dad looked up into the starry night, inhaled the crisp evening air. He noticed the Milky Way streak across the dark sky like fresh fallen snow. "What an enchanting night," he said.

The next week, Dad took the family to beautiful Lake Naivasha in the Masai Mara, the same location where naturalist author Joy Adamson wrote her stories about lions in the 1960s. *Born Free,* the most famous of her books, became a successful movie of the same title. Tamara beamed with excitement but wanted to see the lions. Dad roared again. The car erupted with giggles.

The lake, in a serene, picturesque environment like Walden Pond, created a calm influence over them. More than 400 species of birds migrated into the area after the rainy season. The lake housed a sizable population of hippos. To reach the lodge, they took a ferry to Crescent Island in the center of the lake.

Dad held Tamara in his arms when they exited the boat. He looked up, saw an eagle circle the lake. His arm followed the bird like a rifle. Tamara mimicked her Papa, pointed her arm up too. He kissed her cheek in adoration. Purple swamp hens, whiskered terns, white egrets sailed across the surface of the crystal blue lake, preyed on fish.

They meandered around the lakeshore along a marked path. The three adults watched Tamara stop, touch the simplest elements of nature in wonderment. She tickled a giant crusted bug in the moist soil, put her nose up to a beautiful yellow flower, inhaled the sweet fragrance.

The day went well until Tamara walked into a path of vicious black marching ants, each the size of her pinky finger. Within seconds, hundreds of them climbed up her legs, bit her body. She screamed like an ambulance siren. Dad grabbed her, pulled off her clothes. Mom grabbed each flung article of clothing, turned it inside out, gave it a vigorous shake to remove the ants. After a few minutes, Tamara calmed down, but a lot of bugs bit her. She stayed good-natured. After she dressed, she re-engaged with nature on the dirt trail like nothing happened.

When they left Crescent Island the next day, Tamara walked into another ant army. At three and a half years old, she didn't notice. Soon after they boarded the small rowboat, she let out another scream. More ants bit her. She jumped up, danced what looked like a childish version of hip-hop, rocked the boat from side to side. The boat operator yelled, "Everyone sit, boat will tip over, hippos will eat us!" Dad helped him steady the boat, while Terri and Mom stripped off her clothes. Fifteen minutes later, they made it to shore. Poor Tamara, covered with hundreds of ant bites, looked forlorn.

From Lake Naivasha, they drove east toward Mara Safari Lodge. Actor William Holden, who frequented Kenya in his day, founded this magnificent property near the Tanzanian border. Many well-known guests, like Winston Churchill, Bing Crosby, vacationed there with their families. The torrential rains created spring-like conditions; wildlife roamed along the highway. Baby gazelle flitted to keep up with their grazing mothers. Herds of wildebeests stared back, like they posed for photos against the rustic countryside. A pack of sleek black hyenas fed their young while they picked on an old kill left by lions or other big cats.

Dad spotted a shadow ahead on the road, slowed. Soon the shadow morphed into a lone lion, his muscular seven-foot body sprawled across the middle of the road, a perfect place to sun himself. His presence on the narrow road blocked the car from passing without driving into the dirt gulley. Tamara shook with excitement when Dad told her he put the lion there to let her see a real live lion. He lifted his foot off the brake. The car rolled closer to the lion. His royal mane, like a fur collar, fluttered in the warm breeze. The lion stared at the car, yawned. Tamara said, "He's my lion!" She believed her grandpa put it there for her.

A couple of minutes passed, but the king of the jungle refused to budge. Dad wanted to get to their destination, didn't want to wait for this prima donna lion to move. He honked the horn. Nothing. He honked longer, pressed the horn hard. Dad decided the lion must be deaf, because he refused to move. They stayed in the car for fear of attack. For ten minutes Dad honked, the car crept forward. Tamara's lion stood up on all fours, faced the car, let out a huge roar, moseyed off the road. Laughter filled the car. Tamara glowed because she saw "her" lion.

Spectacular green hillsides like golf course fairways made a stunning backdrop for this luxurious Mara Safari Lodge, a five-star resort in the wild.

However, we never expected the monkey business around the lodge. When Terri and Tamara stepped out of the back seat, a hairy baboon grabbed Tamara's hand. Terri grabbed

Tamara's other hand, she began a tug-of-war with the aggressive baboon. Tamara didn't react with fear. She thought the baboon wanted to make friends. Terri yelled for Dad, who ran around the car, stomped his feet, shouted at the baboon. The disappointed baboon ran off into the bushes. Dad picked up Tamara, didn't let her out of his arms until they got inside the lodge.

Dad checked in, told the story to the hotel clerk. He replied in an elite Kenyan accent, "Sneaky packs of baboons find ways to get in the rooms too. Like hoodlums, they steal people's belongings. Kenyan law forbids us to shoot or cage them. We put up with them."

All four of them enjoyed the magnificent sunset from the open veranda. The sun set, the mushroom-shaped acacia trees distinctive to Kenya became silhouetted against the water-colored sky. Big game often attacked with no notice. Uniformed guards patrolled, to give guests and staff security when on safari.

After dinner, Dad and Mom walked Tamara and Terri to their room on the west side. After he closed the door, Dad listened to make sure Terri turned the lock. He escorted Mom around the corner back to their room. After he brushed his teeth, he said, "I need to check on something. I'll return soon."

He didn't want to alarm Mom, kept his cool. He walked around the building in thick grass, frowned at the open louver window on the side of Terri and Tamara's room.

"Terri, it's Dad."

Terri, in the middle of helping Tamara get into her pajamas, gasped. The intruder in the window startled her. She relaxed when she recognized Dad's voice.

"Lots of monkey business around here today," he said, "I want you to keep these windows fastened shut all night because I don't trust the baboons."

Terri agreed to follow Dad's wishes. They all slept in safety under the African stars.

26

ACTIVE RETIREMENT

In July 1982, Dad said goodbye to the wilds of Kenya. He finished the challenge, wrote curriculum to teach English over the radio. Dad's AIE Team gave Kenyans a solid foundation to become literate in English, enabled future Kenyans to compete in the modern world. Dad and Mom boarded the plane in Nairobi, knew they'd never return to this magnificent country, but also knew they'd carry the cherished memories of these two years in their hearts forever.

On the way home to Northridge, Dad arranged a detour to the exotic city of Rabat, Morocco, in northern Africa. Dad's friend Mike Pavlos, Headmaster at the American International School in Rabat, and his wife Cindy invited them to visit at summer break.

In spite of the heat, they enjoyed the cloth-covered bazaars of Rabat. Although similar in concept to the shops in Kabul, Moroccan *souks* did business in a more modern fashion. Attractive hand-sewn carpets, clothing filled the stalls. Many shops displayed stylish knockoffs of famous French and Italian designers.

On the third day, the Pavlos' took them to Marrakesh, a two-hour drive away. Mike and Cindy guided them through the ancient city, regaled them with tales from medieval times. My father added historical tidbits of his own.

Dad strolled along the narrow labyrinthine paths, studied the detailed architecture of Marrakesh. He imagined the vast sweep of events in Marrakesh over the last twelve centuries. Armies of thousands marched through, wiped out strong empires. For many years, Marrakesh was a sultan's paradise, hosted a rest stop for caravans of thousands. Great musicians performed concerts in open cobblestone squares. Artisans sculpted metals and clay, sold their handicrafts to anyone who wanted to buy.

Dad snapped out of his reverie when Mike and Cindy led them into a famous old restaurant in the medina, each room more ornate than the next. Enormous gilded doors opened to cathedral ceilings. Stained-glass windows sparkled like kaleidoscopes; exotic aromas tantalized their taste buds. Cross-legged, they relaxed on oversized silk cushions while Mike ordered for everyone. Golden platters of fish, lamb, rice, vegetables soon graced the table, a feast fit for kings and queens.

The next day, on the flight home to Los Angeles, Dad thought long and hard about his future.

A week later, he let the Los Angeles Unified School District know he planned to retire after twenty-nine years of service. At fifty-seven in good health, he wanted to open a new chapter in his life. For the first time, he held no tangible goals. Dad knew he wanted to travel more with Mom, yet also wanted to sit back on his own terms, enjoy his home, pool, garden purchased in 1965, his oasis in the suburbs of Los Angeles.

In the first few days back home, Dad realized one of his greatest pleasures, to savor his morning coffee, read the entire *Los Angeles Times* cover to cover. When he worked, he took little time, breezed through the cover stories, caught the rankings of his favorite teams in the Sports section before he drove to his office.

He fell into a routine, unpack two sets of boxes, those shipped from Kenya, another huge pile recovered from the storage facility. One box from Kenya contained Mom's prized carved ivory collection. He left it for her to unwrap because she spent joyous hours hand-selecting them during the two-year stay.

Like most men, Dad loved to organize his garage. A "DIY" (do it yourself) guy around the house, he unwrapped his garage tools like a walk down memory lane. With a crooked grin he remembered the three sets of bedroom furniture he built for each of us kids. Later, we turned one of the small dressers into a storage cabinet in the pool cabana, donated the rest of the furniture to friends.

Some days he trimmed plants in the yard. In the backyard, he created a vegetable garden, planted dwarf fruit trees, peaches, plums, apricots, oranges, lemons. He built a walk-in greenhouse from old windows from the house.

Dad relished the undisturbed freedom to read while he ate lunch. Novels, biographies, news publications became his passion. After a couple of weeks, he reminded himself, "I'm retired. I don't need to rush back to work. I can take the whole afternoon, read if I feel like it. I can even take a nap."

To adapt to retired life, he and Mom agreed how they'd handle meals. She fixed dinner any night of the week, he made his own breakfast and lunch. A creature of habit, he ate a bowl of hot oatmeal six mornings a week, cornflakes with cold milk on the seventh. Dad's not big on salads. For lunch he fixed a salami sandwich or munched on leftovers. Mom made it easy for him, sealed the leftovers in marked plastic containers.

For their entire married life, Mom awakened first. She made coffee, brought in the newspaper, filled in part of the daily crossword puzzle. Dad gained great satisfaction when he completed the puzzle. This understated camaraderie, among the many simple rituals they developed when newlyweds, carried forward for sixty-five years.

In Kenya, Dad told Mom he'd like to purchase a motor home, drive around North America. Mom agreed with the idea. At the end of their first week home, she noticed the neighbor across the street posted a "for sale" sign on their motor home, mentioned it to Dad. In the afternoon, Dad strolled over, returned twenty minutes later the proud owner of the home on wheels. The neighbor, who only used the vehicle three times, included the home goods she stocked in the motor home.

Dad checked out travel books from the library, subscribed to *Sunset* magazine, planned road trips.

He also needed practice, drove the motor home around town while he ran errands. He even drove it to eat dinner with their close friends, Patti and Roland Faucher, who lived only two miles away. Roland and Patti managed our home property, collected rent, arranged repairs while Dad worked in both Afghanistan and Kenya. After dinner, Dad felt grateful for such loyal friends. They exchanged goodbyes, he and Mom buckled up, he started the over-sized vehicle's engine. Instead of driving around the block to head home, he did a three-point turn, smashed the Faucher's curbside mailbox. For years Roland and Patti teased him about his shoddy driving skills.

Over the next few months, they took several trial road trips in California. Their first long-distance caravan, up the West Coast into British Columbia with Cal and Ruth Gray, tennis buddies of Dad's. The Grays drove their own motor home to give each couple plenty of private time. Dad used his navigational skills to plan how many miles to drive each day, which campgrounds to stay in each evening. Due to weather and sightseeing, he recalculated this plan daily with his trusty guidebook.

They entered Canada by ferry from Washington State to Victoria, on Vancouver Island. Dad flashed back to his Air Force Reserve days, when he marveled at the western United States and Canadian coastlines from the air in C130s on his way to Anchorage, Alaska. He remembered the vastness of the United States, impossible to depict on a mere book map. Now, he drove through the region, appreciated the grandeur of the North American coast from ground level.

They made it a habit to wander off the beaten track into small towns for lunch. Old guys in rockers played checkers outside a storefront, a familiar scene. From the stares they received, they felt like an entourage of celebrities rolling into town. The towns seemed stuck in a time warp, reminded Dad of St. Louis back in the thirties, complete with soda shops and fresh salt-water taffy. He also enjoyed bakeries.

"I love to walk in, smell fresh breads, see a display of delicious desserts," he said.

They often purchased scrumptious treats at these stores to complete their evening meals at local campgrounds. Every day at four o'clock, they got off the road, settled in, drank a cocktail, grilled up tasty morsels for dinner. Dad handled the grill, Mom prepared the rest of the meal.

Outside of Victoria, they watched thousands of Coho salmon jump the white crested rapids on their way upriver to spawn. Dad heard the rush of the icy blue water, felt a surge of adrenaline.

Back from the three-week trip to Canada, Dad played tennis to get fit, swam in the backyard pool, cultivated his garden. He and Mom attended live theatre several times a month, became season ticket holders at the Ahmanson Theater in Los Angeles. If the show sparked their interest, they added performances at the Dorothy Chandler Pavilion. Although Dad loved the music, he told Mom the drive through Los Angeles traffic bothered him. They needed to find smaller, local theatres to support.

They discovered excellent shows at the Pasadena Playhouse. There they met many people who also attended regular performances. After he booked tickets one day, Dad remarked to Mom, "This theatre first presented burlesque back in 1912, transformed the community of Pasadena into the largest art center in the state of California." He added, "Celebrated actors like Dustin Hoffman, Ernest Borgnine, Raymond Burr, Gene Hackman, Sally Struthers all trained at this playhouse."

Although my father enjoyed the comforts of home, within months he itched to go on another adventure in their RV. They discussed a trip to the East Coast with Clyde and Arnita Millett, tennis buddies and educators who also owned a home on wheels. He looked forward to the brilliant East Coast autumn colors, prominent in early October.

Their first noteworthy stop on the cross-country trip came at the Air Force Academy in Colorado Springs. Dad flashed his Lieutenant Colonel I. D. card. The gate guard waved him through.

A warm rush of emotion hit Dad when he visited the barracks and the Air Force planes, talked with new cadets. His mind flashed back to his own military training in the 1940's, when he pushed his body, mind, spirit to the limit, enjoyed each new challenge placed in front of him.

Now in his late fifties, the scene fascinated my father. On a warm, sunny October day on the Colorado plains, he watched cadets parachute out of planes, aim for the big white X in the open field. A group of cadets performed strategic maneuvers in gliders, while others participated in various team sports. Dad watched the new recruits prepare for important duties to serve our nation and its citizens.

Sunday morning, my parents opted to attend a Christian church with the Millets, who liked to explore new churches on vacation. They never proselytized, respected Dad and Mom's Jewish beliefs. At a famous cathedral built in the late 1800's, Dad entered the historic house of God in a somber mood. He gazed up at the magnificent stained-glass windows, saw sunshine beam in from all directions, rainbows of color like a disco ball. He whispered, "This colorful glass makes us feel like we're in a life-size kaleidoscope." They all agreed, inhaled the glory of the morning worship. Afterwards, to tease Dad's agnosticism, Clyde said, "God beamed the light upon us." They chuckled. After the service, Dad treated everyone to brunch at the Officer's Club on base.

Overnight, the weather in the mountains turned ominous. Morrie became concerned with the dark clouds. The next morning, on the drive north to Denver, a blizzard caught them, a total whiteout! Clyde trailed close behind until Dad turned into a Wal-Mart parking lot. The wind howled around them. Dad parked the motor home front into the wind to make sure it wouldn't blow over. Clyde, unaware of the danger, parked his vehicle perpendicular to the wind. Dad radioed, "Repark, stay close together." Due to poor visibility, they didn't move for the rest of the night.

They awoke to a foot of fresh powder. Dad recalculated their route, headed across the Great Plains to Kansas. Along the highway, a sign advertised the Eisenhower Presidential Library. They spent several hours among the one-of-kind exhibits.

They continued east through Middle America. Clyde suggested they spend their nights in church parking lots rather than look for trailer parks. The idea pleased Dad. It saved them time, allowed them to walk around the small towns, meet the locals. But in small towns, men carried rifles slung over their shoulders like purses. The four travelers feared robbery or attack and stuck together.

To break up the monotonous drive, they often stopped at a park or high school, where my father played tennis with Clyde. The exercise felt good, relieved the tedium.

When they arrived in Buffalo, New York, the city's condition shocked Dad, houses for sale, many abandoned, store windows boarded up.

Dad struck up a conversation with the dowdy cashier in a run-down food market. She said most of the manufacturers in Buffalo, a vibrant, middle class city, relocated to cities in the south, where fewer unions made labor costs cheaper. In 1984, Dad knew in his heart he looked at a portent of things to come. He read about the trend for people to leave cities in the Northeast, head for Sunbelt cities in the Southwest, where more plentiful jobs, more enjoyable weather awaited them.

They awoke early the next morning ready to visit Niagara Falls and Canada. Dad remembered flying over the great falls once on an Air Force run. When he peered down from the sightseeing ledge, he found the churning water hypnotic, felt the cool spray on his face, shielded the rest of his body with a yellow hooded slicker given out to tourists. The exhilaration of the clean verdant water gave Dad a thrill.

The most vivid rainbow he ever saw appeared above the falls. While Dad didn't believe in God, he appreciated how Mother Nature staged the scene.

They spent a couple of days in Toronto, another night in Montreal. Dad's love for history showed up again when he recounted stories of the French and Indian Wars. While they strolled through the town, took in the memorials, Dad brought historical chronicles to life, which added flavor to their sightseeing.

He recalled, "In 1689, the British Army aided the Iroquois Tribe in the worst massacre of the new French colony."

The modern city of Toronto, different from the splendid architectural detail of the older city of Montreal, astounded him.

Faye and Morrie on their 40th anniversary

The weather turned wet. When they reentered the United States through New York, Dad caught a miserable cold. Instead of playing tourist in Massachusetts and Connecticut, they headed south to Alexandria, Virginia, where they arranged a visit with Tony and Camille Lanza, good friends from Kabul, Afghanistan.

Camille organized all the details. She coordinated with the doctor across the street to let Clyde and Arnita park, plug in their motor home. Mom and Dad parked in the Lanza's driveway.

Three days later, Dad recovered from his cold, so, with the Lanza's, they drove to pick up Aunt Tamara, Mom's sister, who flew in from Oakland, CA. A widow for the second time, she felt safe with Mom and Dad while she returned to the mainstream of life after she lost my Uncle Sol. Together, they spent Columbus Day weekend in Lancaster, Pennsylvania, in Amish country. On the drive from Virginia, Dad fed everyone historical treats.

"Large numbers of Amish faced religious persecution from Protestants and Catholics, took up William Penn's offer of religious freedom in this region in the early 1700s, which gave the state of Pennsylvania its name," he said.

When bedtime arrived, all five adults, except Clyde and Arnita, slept in my parents' motor home. They strung a blanket for privacy like in the old Hollywood movie *It Happened One Night* with Clark Gable and Claudette Colbert. After lots of giggles, they acknowledged the fun day, fell fast asleep.

The next few days they toured our nation's capital, then Virginia landmarks. Dad learned new facts at Monticello, Thomas Jefferson's estate. A brass plaque noted a Commodore Levy owned Monticello after Jefferson's death. Nobody mentioned this, which he found strange. Dad raced to the local library to check out this odd fact.

At the time, a Jewish Naval Commodore named Levy lived in town. When Jefferson died, he owed a large amount of money, the estate became run down. Commodore Levy, with high regard for Jefferson, paid the debt, refurbished the estate with his own money. Commodore Levy saved Monticello, a historic monument viewed by hundreds of thousands of visitors every year.

From Virginia, they made their way down the East Coast to the Walt Disney resort in Orlando, Florida, then to Cape Canaveral, where Dad arranged for V.I.P. seats to observe a space shuttle liftoff.

In the darkness before dawn, energy buzzed from the crowd in the bleachers. One group carried American flags, others wore red, white and blue clothes to display their patriotism, honor the moment in history they waited to witness.

All eyes focused on the monstrous metal missile perched three miles away. The crowd chanted, "Ten! Nine! Eight!" Louder. "Seven! Six! Five!"

A man to Dad's right shouted, "Main engine start!"

Dad focused hard on the launch pad on the horizon. It looked like a still photograph. His memory raced back to July 24, 1969, when he joined the glass hallway greeting line to welcome home Apollo 11 astronauts Neil Armstrong, Buzz Aldrin, Michael Collins from the first moonwalk. Seconds passed. Three! Two! One! He held his breath, the crowd waited in silence.

Bursts of orange flamed out from the external fuel tank. White clouds billowed up around the scaffold. Dad thought about the four astronauts on board, their courage, their vulnerability.

A fierce sound erupted from the solid rocket boosters. The bleachers rumbled, shook like an earthquake. Dad felt the vibration in his bones. The colossal rocket lifted, cheers rang out, the fiery vessel lit up the sky. They watched in utter amazement, until the trail of light faded out of view.

27

RETURNING TO EDUCATION

Morrie, a pioneer in technology, joined the PLATO Society at his alma mater, UCLA, a new high-level Learning in Retirement (LIR) program with research and discussion groups. He found the discussions, which featured important topics, great fun. He interacted with retired professionals, attorneys, doctors, CPAs, engineers, physicists, professors, a few artists, writers, producers, directors, actors in this unique group. I loved to see Dad on an intellectual high.

He attended PLATO on a weekly basis. After two years, a traffic jam caused my father to arrive late. He berated himself. Ridiculous, took an hour and a half to drive twenty miles to

Westwood. At age sixty-five, he decided not to drive this route another ten or twenty years.

The idea struck like a jolt of electricity. He lived three blocks from a great university. Why not start an LIR at California State University, Northridge?

Dad checked out PLATO's history. PLATO began with a $200,000 grant from UCLA. After one year of planning, the first discussion group included fifteen people. In two short years, the group grew to 300 members. Francis Meyers, one of the members, developed a book on how to start LIR programs. Dad treated him to a deli lunch one afternoon. Over a pastrami sandwich, he learned the process.

The next week, Francis handed Dad a floppy disk with the entire contents of his handbook. Dad raced off on his next quest, oozed with excitement.

Early in the fall of 1986, Dad mailed a letter to Dr. Cleary, the President of CSUN, requested a meeting to discuss a new LIR on campus for seniors in the San Fernando Valley. November rolled around, no response. Dad phoned Dr. Cleary's secretary, who formerly worked in the PLATO office at UCLA. Numerous phone calls transpired between them. Because of Dad's charm, great sense of humor, the two became fast friends. She assured my father Dr. Cleary did in fact receive his letter. Dad decided not to bother him until after the holidays.

On January 4, 1987, Dad began to call every Monday, which demonstrated persistence pays off. By the second Monday in February, the secretary informed Dad Dr. Cleary handed his letter to one of the Vice Presidents, who walked out the door with it.

Fifteen minutes later, the phone rang. My father arranged a lunch appointment with Sonja Marchand, the Director of Business Education in the Extended Learning Division. This luncheon sparked **S**tudy, **A**ctivity, **G**rowth, and **E**nrichment, also called SAGE.

Morrie speaking at SAGE

Recharged with a new purpose, Dad put together an exceptional team of faculty, deans, selected retirees to meet at his house to develop SAGE. Sonja offered to loan SAGE $1,500 from the Extension Division fund, but Dad needed more.

"Cutler Luck" materialized again when a former colleague from Los Angeles Unified School District, Jules Lesner, called to catch up. Jules left education, became Director of the Milken Foundation.

"The foundation promotes discovery and advancement of inventive, effective ways to help people help themselves, and those around them to lead productive satisfying lives," he said.

When Dad told him about his new project, SAGE, Jules lit up. The next week Jules delivered a check for $15,000. SAGE was born.

In September 1987, Dad welcomed twenty-eight retirees to the first SAGE open house. Most came from word-of-mouth. Half became members ready to participate in the first study group. Morrie appointed himself President/Treasurer, no members opposed the motion. In the small rented room above the CSUN Credit Union, on furniture borrowed from the university warehouse, the initial members began to discuss Supreme Court decisions. Dad loved the intellectual banter. By the end of the ten-week session, SAGE grew to twenty-four members. They made plans for a second study group.

By 1990, Dad and his friend Jerry Eisen established "Senior Computer," an auxiliary program of SAGE. They worked out a deal with the Information and Technology Department at CSUN to use the computer lab for six weeks between school sessions in both summer and winter.

He enjoyed the novelty of personal computers. Email and the Internet didn't exist. Dad worked with Jerry on the cutting edge to help seniors move into the twenty-first century. My father wrote a computer handbook for students, taught a class on word processing. He and Jerry posted simple flyers at public libraries around the Valley.

Within the first year, dozens of people joined waiting lists for classes. Computers became more sophisticated. They added email and the World Wide Web to the curriculum. Dad, Jerry, and Leon, another gifted teacher, taught the computer classes. They recruited eight volunteers who tutored the classrooms of senior students, many their first exposure to computers.

Morrie and Faye in China

When Dad didn't plan or teach for SAGE, he and Mom traveled to exotic places around the world. He subscribed to various travel magazines, cut out reviews of possible destinations, out of the way hotels, fabulous restaurants, fun excursions. One day, I snooped for Dad's candy stash (tootsie rolls, red vines, jellybeans), ran across an entire drawer of his file cabinet devoted to travel, his personal travel library.

Morrie and Faye in Central America

Morrie at Elder Hostel in China

Their trips grew in frequency. I wanted to attach electronic trackers to my parents to keep up with their location in the world. Dad's favorite destinations included China, Hong Kong, Italy, France, an archeological dig in Utah. Along the way, they discovered Elder Hostel (now called Road Scholar), which conducted educational vacations for adults. Dad *lived with purpose*, soaked up adventure, gave back to others in his community, high on life.

Faye in China

My father acted like Superman, from the childhood comic books he read. Then, toward the end of 1997, he discovered he was human. After he and Mom returned home from a tropical excursion to Central America, Dad felt lethargic. The day before they left Belize, Dad scuba dived for the first time, at age seventy-three, loved it. He functioned in low gear, pushed himself through daily tasks.

Morrie at the Great Wall

Several days passed, but the problem refused to go away. My father never wanted to go to the doctor. However, with coaxing from Mom, he agreed to seek answers.

The doctor ran a series of tests, sent him home to rest. When the doctor called with the results, Dad got his wakeup call. He had a bladder infection, hypertension, prostate cancer. What a jolt! The big "C" awakened many depressive thoughts. His son Wayne died of a brain tumor; his brother Alex died of liver cancer. Was this his fate?

Startled into disbelief, Dad decided to remain optimistic, not let fear overtake him. His doctors began radiation treatment. Yet, like everyone diagnosed with cancer, the unknown causes concern. He followed the doctors' orders, stayed active every day. Jerry Eisen met Dad at the gym three times a week. This gave my father the motivation to continue. Exhausted like an old workhorse, most days he returned home, ate lunch, took a nap. Teaching his classes at SAGE also gave him a reason to drag himself out of bed. His energy diminished each day. Most of his students never knew about his illness, because Dad never shared, never complained, not his style.

The next year, at 74 years of age, he celebrated. His medical tests showed no trace of the ugly cancer. Dad again looked forward to life. For him, cancer turned into hiccups, a minor inconvenience. He continued to gallop through life like a seasoned thoroughbred.

SAGE continued to grow in popularity. More seniors around the San Fernando Valley became members. Since its inception in 1987 the SAGE Society awarded hundreds of thousands of dollars in scholarships to students of CSUN. Dad enjoyed his busy retirement years, satisfied his efforts helped seniors lead more stimulating lives in retirement. He was delighted the membership fund provided assistance to worthy students of CSUN.

28

ALTRUISM

While Dad orchestrated SAGE, my parents helped relocate the Tarin family to the San Fernando Valley. Hadji Tarin served as lead writer with Dad at the Ministry of Education in Kabul, Afghanistan.

Eight years after the Soviet invasion in 1978, when the Taliban took over, life in Kabul became unbearable. For Hadji, a prominent educator tasked to modernize the Afghan educational system, ensure the preservation of core, centuries-old Afghan values, to remain in Kabul meant certain death. He, his wife Latifa, their six children fled their war-ravaged homeland. Hadji knew if the Taliban captured his family, they'd kill them all. They dressed like Kuchi nomads to hide their identities.

The family made a long, perilous escape from tyranny, crossed the Hindu Kush Mountains through the treacherous Khyber Pass on foot, a frightful experience. To lighten the task, Hadji shared stories with his children of the beautiful land they sought to become part of.

First, they lived in tent camps outside of Peshawar, Pakistan, with tens of thousands of other Afghan refugees. Hadji and his family reached Islamabad, where he found a teaching job. While he worked there, Hadji and Latifa discussed where to begin a new life with their family. Hadji traveled to the United States while he did educational research for the Afghan government in the 1970s. America remained foremost on his list. The way Americans accepted his faith resonated for him during his three-week visit. He established friendships he never imagined possible, with people of different faiths, cultures, skin colors. He marveled at the welcoming nature of the American people. In 1973 he didn't know in a matter of three decades, he'd choose the United States to be his adopted homeland.

It took Hadji about a year to find Morrie's address through another former colleague in New York. When Dad received the petition from Hadji to sponsor his family in the United States, he reflected on how his own parents Abe and Bella emigrated from Russia, their gratitude for the freedom they found in the United States. My father paid it forward to Hadji's family, who wanted to make the world a better place for others. My father, born in America, knew the sensational opportunities available to the Tarins. True to his nature, Dad resolved to help.

My parents picked up the entire family at LAX airport in two cars, welcomed them into our home for eight days, until a three-bedroom apartment became available in the West Valley.

All wore Afghan attire, including the *chadris* and head cover worn by the women.

Morrie and Faye 50th anniversary

Mom called everyone she knew to ask for donations. My sister Terri put the word out to her network too. Loads of used articles arrived at my parents' address. Within a few days, the garage filled with furniture, boxes of housewares, linens. Since they knew the ages and genders of each child, everyone guessed at sizes for clothes. His friends' generosity elated Dad.

Mom helped Latifa make the apartment a real home, stocked the refrigerator with fresh food. Latifa hyperventilated on her first visit to the grocery store when she saw the array of choices.

Dad, their official sponsor, enrolled everyone in school. The oldest children and parents attended free English classes at Valley Skill Center.

For the first time, I realized people from a wide range of educational institutions recognized my father. The head counselor at the Skill Center greeted Dad like an old friend, gave special attention to the Tarins. Haris, the youngest, only eight, enrolled in public school right away. These bright, eager friends learned English. After a year, they functioned well in their new country.

The eldest children searched for work, enrolled in community college, while the others attended Reseda High

School. Latifa learned to not bargain while shopping at supermarkets, allowed her children to take on Western ways. Hadji spent his days at the mosque, enjoyed many visitors. A respected teacher in Kabul, scores of his students in Southern California came to honor him in the house of Allah. Like many immigrants, they adapted, made a memorable mark in their new community.

Hadji and Morrie, Muslim and Jew, shared mutual respect. Together they identified with common core values of family and education, searched for ideas to create a brighter tomorrow.

Several years later, Hadji passed away. My father mourned the loss of his dear friend. Yet, through Hadji's teaching, an unconditional bond lives on in Hadji's children, grandchildren. They sought my father's wisdom for decades, called him their Godfather.

29

THE FINAL STAIRWAY

In his twilight years, Dad acknowledged new mountains to climb: shaky knees, achy back, sputtering memory. Doctors diagnosed angiosarcoma, a rare malignant cancer of the scalp. The dermatologist said this form of cancer attacks mainly elderly white men.

Dad did not dispute the seriousness of the prognosis. He maintained a calm acceptance, surrendered to the situation, placed his focus on solutions. He refused to give up. He faced the facts head-on, wondered, "Is this how I bow out?"

Much like the program to treat his prostate cancer, the radiologist prescribed an aggressive thirty-day radiation treatment, five days a week for six weeks. He drove to Kaiser Hospital on Sunset Boulevard in Los Angeles in morning rush-hour traffic. Some days, Mom rode with him to allow him to drive in the carpool lane. On other days, Dad's friends alternated to keep him company.

In his first two weeks of radiation therapy, my father found plenty of time to think. Dad learned unwavering values like honesty, pride, a strong work ethic, and the importance of family from his uneducated immigrant parents during the Great Depression. He also learned neither God nor life guaranteed an easy journey. One works to fulfill the highest, truest expression of oneself.

He reflected on his good fortune to become an officer in the Army Air Corps during World War II, his ticket out of St. Louis, Missouri. Each mission he flew gained him respect for elite equipment and life itself. Wartime sparked his thirst for adventure.

In his ninetieth year, Morrie lived an extraordinary life, iconic, like a Hollywood classic. His heart swelled at thoughts of his beautiful wife Faye, his two loving daughters. Blessed with true friends, able to continue a comfortable lifestyle, he felt full. He read newspapers, books, magazines, part of his daily ritual. He relished his life experiences, took more pleasure from teaching than all the recognition he amassed in his illustrious career. He awoke each day with a renewed sense of curiosity and eternal optimism, believed each person is born with the ability to unleash the potential within to develop his or her unique talents. He made significant achievements in education, remained relatable, relational, and relevant. Using words and deeds, he gave millions a chance to lead productive lives.

The prologue highlights one young Afghan woman who learned to read from his textbooks as an impoverished refugee and as a result was accepted into college in the United States, where her life will be far richer.

These physical testaments of his compassion and dedication exemplify all the historical narratives we may never know about people whose lives were enriched by this one man who loved educating people. We can only guess the impact my father had among generations of Afghans, Kenyans, and Californians alike.

Education, the inalienable right of children, unlocks the door to mindful awareness, the freedom to think, explore, discover, create and change our world. Imagination and innovation is our classroom to teach what is possible.

Morris Cutler, a genuine superhero, humanitarian, life enricher, created a better world for generations to come.

MORRIS CUTLER SCHOLARSHIP FUND

EDUCATION WARRIORS

A Non-Profit Organization

Every child deserves a quality education. Education unites the world. We're all warriors at heart, and collectively, we CAN make a difference.

In honor of Morris Cutler, I created a non-profit, **Education Warriors** to provide tutoring scholarships to deserving youth from all backgrounds.

The more money we raise, the more students get academic assistance.

Your generous donation, whether $10 or $10,000, empowers students to stay in school, go to college, and build a better tomorrow.

"Be the change you wish to see in the world." Gandhi

To donate go to
www.EducationWarrior.org

Made in the USA
Columbia, SC
24 March 2022